A DAD'S GUIDE TO ADULTING

HOW TO START YOUR INDEPENDENT LIFE

A DAD'S GUIDE TO ADULTING:

HOW TO START YOUR INDEPENDENT LIFE

Robert J Petty

First Edition: May 2024

Cover Design © 2024 by Kelsey Petty

Graphics © 2024 by Kelsey Petty

ISBN 979-8-218-40067-5

Robert Petty Publishing

PRAISE FOR A DAD'S GUIDE TO ADULTING

"A Dad's Guide To Adulting is a concise, yet informative reference for anyone starting out on their own. It's easy to read and explains many buzz words in simple to understand language. This would make a great required course for anyone preparing to enter our economic society on their own. Great, unbiased, practical advice from a well-seasoned Dad on how to navigate the stage of adulthood with confidence and success!"

-- Rebecca S.

"This book would make a wonderful graduation gift for teens just getting out of high school or college. Coming from a generation when parents didn't even teach young adults how to write a check, I can only wish I had access to a how-to manual this informative back then. It's concise, educational, and very well written. Kudos to the author for shedding a light on all things 'adulting!'"

-- Jeri T.

"Written from a father's perspective, this is a handy, concise guide for young people starting out on their own. It's packed with practical, useful information on a variety of real-world matters ranging from where to begin, to pitfalls to avoid. It is well-organized for ready reference as needed, with just the right amount of detail. It's the kind of information many of us wish we had when we were young."

-- Dan P.

To my wife, Benita,

and my kids, Jillian, Kelsey, and Jackson.

You give me purpose, and opportunities to learn.

TABLE OF CONTENTS

ACKNOWLEDGMENTS

Special thanks to the following people for their assistance in getting this book published:

Rachel Petty for taking on the arduous task of cleaning up my many typos and grammatical gaffs.

Jeri Beatty Thomas for more copy editing and style assistance.

Benita Petty for copy editing and design assistance.

Kelsey Petty for cover art and interior graphics design.

Bruce Petty for content accuracy editing.

1 INTRODUCTION

I've heard the phrase from newly independent young adults, "Adulting is hard." Obviously, this is in reference to the many things we all must navigate as adults that we never even had to think about in our parents' homes. I have three adult children and through the transition from childhood to adulthood, I observed how many things they needed to learn to live on their own. Most of these things are second nature for those of us who have been doing it for a while. If we were taught them at all, we either learned it from our parents, just like I had to teach my kids along the way, or we learned it the hard way. Unfortunately, learning these things the hard way often means paying penalties for doing them late or not at all.

As more and more of these instances arose where my own children missed certain steps along the way, it occurred to me that someone needed to write a book on the topic. So why not me?

Whenever someone writes a guidebook on any subject, we want to know their credentials. In other words, why should I listen to them? Well, as the title indicates, my first credential is that I'm a dad, so I can lean on that experience. But I have some other educational, work, and life experiences that contributed to my general knowledge of the topics covered in this guide.

I've been a(n):

- Accountant
- CPA
- Real Estate Agent
- Mortgage Loan Officer
- Life Insurance Agent

Robert Petty

But much of my knowledge on these topics comes from experience through buying and selling homes, remodeling homes, purchasing and selling vehicles, performing vehicle self-maintenance, investing, handling workplace benefits for my family, and so on.

I do not claim to be more qualified to write on these topics than some other writers. I recommend you supplement this guide with additional reading on any topic where you feel you need more detailed information.

My purpose for writing this is to put these common adulting tasks in one place in an easy-to-digest format. This guide is not intended to be comprehensive, and it cannot be specific to the laws of every state or locality. It is intended to be a general guide for those entering adulthood so they are less likely to miss important steps along the way.

I hope you will find this guide helpful. If you find yourself still confused about any item in this guide, feel free to send your questions my way at robertjpetty59@gmail.com. I will do my best to provide additional information to help you.

2 BANKING

C hecking accounts – whether you choose an online bank or a conventional bank with branches, you will need a checking account, even if you never write a check. Checking accounts are required by your employer for direct deposit of your paycheck. You will also need a debit card to make purchases at both physical and online stores. Debit cards are usually linked directly to a checking account rather than a savings account.

Whether using an online or conventional bank, you will likely be able to open your bank accounts online. Simply create a user account on the bank's website and open your bank accounts there.

Many checking accounts will not have a monthly fee if you maintain a minimum balance or have at least one direct deposit per month. Be sure to look for a free account if possible. There is no need to eat up your hard-earned money on bank fees.

Also, look for accounts with no overdraft fees. Overdraft fees are charges your bank levies if you spend more than you have in your bank account. These fees can add up quickly if you make a mistake. If you are unable to get an account with no overdraft fees, you can usually attach your checking account to a credit card or a savings account where the needed funds can be accessed when an overdraft occurs. Even if the bank charges a fee for the overdraft transfer, the fee is typically far less than the overdraft fee.

If you like having some cash with you, also be sure to look for a bank with several ATM locations, or a bank that reimburses you the fees for using other banks' ATMs. Many online banks have agreements with conventional banks to allow their customers to use their ATMs.

> Tip: Setup alerts on your bank's website for things like daily balance, prior day transactions, transactions that exceed a particular amount, etc. Alerts will help you detect fraudulent charges very quickly.

Probably every bank has a smart phone app. Familiarize yourself with your bank's app so you know where and how to quickly turn your debit card off and on. If you suspect a fraudulent transaction on your account, instead of immediately cancelling your card, turn your card off temporarily until you've had time to investigate the charge. On several occasions I've thought a charge was fraudulent but it turned out to just be a charge I forgot about or didn't recognize at first. Many times a transaction will appear with a different company name than the company you made a purchase from causing confusion. Another situation is if you have a subscription to a service that has an annual charge. It is easy to forget about a charge that you haven't seen for a full year.

Savings accounts – many banks will help you open a free savings account when you set up a checking account. Savings accounts are like a checking account but are intended to have far less transactions than a checking account. Savings accounts are simply a convenient place to set aside funds for an intended future purpose such as emergencies, vacations, or whatever you need. As with checking accounts, be sure to look for accounts with no fees.

While online bank accounts are great, an account at a conventional bank with a branch near you has some advantages:

- Although many paper checks can be deposited using your smartphone, most all banks have a dollar limit on how much you can deposit this way. When this happens, a local branch is convenient to make your deposit the old-fashioned way.

- Occasionally, you may need to have a document notarized. This is when a person called a notary public is required to witness you signing an important document. After witnessing that it was really you who signed the document, the notary will sign and place their notary seal on the document. This service usually comes with a fee, but if you are a customer at a bank, they will usually provide notary services free.

- Branch banks also provide investment services, home loans, car loans, personal loans, and other services.

3 BUDGETING

Everyone needs a budget. If you are like most people, you will have a limited amount of income (money coming in) to pay your expenses (money going out). Even if the budget is as simple as writing it out on a cocktail napkin, at least you will have some idea if you have enough income to afford apartment A or apartment B, how large of a car payment you can afford, and even how much you have for your daily coffee fix.

Many online tools can assist you with this task if you want to get a bit more formal with your budgeting, and any of these tools will likely be an improvement over the cocktail napkin. One of the biggest benefits of using a computerized budgeting tool is a sample budget that will help you with suggested budget items that you may otherwise overlook. But however you choose to do it, the main thing is that you do it. Without some understanding of your finances, inevitably, you will overspend.

Tip: Set up a reminder on your phone for a once-a-month budget review. By comparing what you planned to spend, to what you actually spent for the month, you'll be able to identify small problems before they become big problems.

To get started on your budget, first figure out how much income you will receive each month. You can find this on a pay slip from one of your previous paychecks. Even if your paycheck is automatically deposited into your bank account by your employer, they will provide you some means of reviewing your paystub through an online portal of some type.

If you get paid other than monthly, such as weekly (once a week), bi-weekly (every two weeks), or semi-monthly (two times per month), be sure to calculate your approximate monthly paycheck for budgeting. Because so many bills are paid once a month (rent, electric, water, etc.), budgets need to be based on monthly amounts.

Because you can only spend what you receive, you need to use the net amount on the paystub, not the gross. "Net" means the amount left after all the deductions are taken.

"Gross" means the total amount before any deductions are subtracted. Deductions are amounts subtracted from your gross pay such as federal and state income taxes, social security taxes, health insurance premiums, 401(k) contributions, etc. Some of these items are mandatory for all U.S. employees such as federal and state taxes, social security, etc., and others are based on items you opt into with your company such as health insurance, short-term disability insurance, 401(k), etc. But regardless of whether they are mandatory or optional, they are deducted from your gross pay.

Next, list your expenses (items you expect to pay each month), starting with the higher items such as rent, utilities (electric, natural gas, water, internet service), renter's insurance, and other items related to your home. Then try to estimate items such as groceries, fuel for your car, dining out, and other items that vary from month-to-month. If you are new to paying many of these expenses yourself, you may need to estimate some of them initially.

Subtract all these expense amounts from the net pay you calculated earlier and pray that there is something left over. If your total expenses are greater than your net pay, you'll have to find places in your budget where you can reduce your spending. This will most likely be discretionary items (items you directly control) like dining out, coffee fixes, streaming services, and the like. Here is a simple example:

My Simple Budget

Income		Budget	Actual	
	Monthly Pay (After Taxes & Deductions)	3,500	3,500	
Expenses				
	Church Contributions	300	300	
	Rent	1,200	1,200	
	Car Payment	300	300	
	Fuel	200	300	Driving to girlfriend's house
	Electric	125	175	Kept house too cold
	Natural Gas	35	35	
	Water	20	20	
	Garbage	25	25	
	Internet	100	100	
	Netflix	20	50	Paid for too many movies
	Hulu	15	15	Paid for too many movies
	Apple TV	20	40	
	Dining	300	500	Got a new girlfriend
	Savings	100	100	
	Miscellaneous	200	400	Got a new girlfriend
	Total Expenses	2,960	3,560	
	Surplus (Deficit)	540	(60)	

Then, each month compare what you spent for each item you budgeted as shown above. You will likely find many differences, especially on the items you had to estimate. In some cases, you'll realize some of your estimates were not realistic, so you will need to adjust them up or down. For example, maybe groceries are way more expensive than you expected, or you had to drive your car a lot more miles than you expected. On the other hand, you may have to adjust your lifestyle to reduce some of your expenses. Maybe you can't eat steak twice a week, or you can take your lunch to work instead of eating out every day. Perhaps you need to limit yourself to one coffee per day from your favorite coffee shop, instead of three! Is there public transportation you can use part of the time to reduce your gasoline use? These are examples of things you can control to bring your spending within your budget.

4 SAVING

Create a budget so you can have something left over to put into savings. In fact, add a savings item to your budget so saving is intentional, not merely accidental.

No matter how small the amount, start saving early and regularly. Even if you don't accumulate a large amount of savings right away, it will get you into the habit of saving.

As your income increases and you find ways to save on other budget items, gradually increase your regular savings amount whenever possible. As you see your savings grow, it will make you want to save more.

Let me point out that this savings is different from retirement savings (to be covered in a later section). This savings is intended to be readily accessible to you for emergencies or other requirements. You can usually open a savings account with no fees at the same time you open a checking account. Refer to the banking section above for more details on bank accounts.

One of the best ways to avoid being forced to use a credit card is to have some sort of emergency fund, even if it is only $1,000. If you have a car repair, a doctor's visit, or some other emergency, having a fund set aside may be enough to pay it so you don't have to use a credit card.

There is no monthly savings amount that is right for everyone. However, your budget should help you understand what is possible for you. As mentioned above, treat your savings amount as a line item in your budget, not as an afterthought or only if you have something leftover. A good rule of thumb is to pick a reasonable percentage, like 5% of your net pay, as a starting place for how much to save.

Tip: Only spend money from your emergency fund for real emergencies, like car repairs, medical expenses, and other unexpected costs. A weekend getaway or splurging on an expensive meal is not an emergency.

5 CREDIT CARDS

A s a dad, my first instinct is to advise against using credit cards entirely, with good reasons:

- Research shows that nearly everyone has overused credit cards at some point in their lives. In fact, according to 2022 data from the Federal Reserve Bank of New York and the U.S. Census Bureau, the average American household owes $7,951 in credit card debt.

- Credit card companies will start filling up your mailbox and inbox with credit card offers as soon as you turn 18. Even without any income, or even a job, credit card companies will try to tempt you to open a credit card account. It may sound like free money, but I assure you, it is not.

- Credit card debt typically carries much higher interest rates than other types of debt like consumer loans or home mortgages. In fact, over the last 10 years, average APR (Annual Percentage Rates) on credit cards almost doubled from 12.9 percent in late 2013 to 22.8 percent in 2023.

- Regardless of how good your interest rate is, if you only make the minimum payments required by the credit card company, you will likely never, yes never, pay off the balance. For example, say you have a credit card account that charges 18% interest, and you have $10,000 in credit card debt. If the minimum payments are equal to interest plus 1% of the balance, it would take 342 months to pay off the debt by making minimum payments alone. That's 28.5 years, and that is if you never added to that

Tip: Set up alerts on your credit card whenever a charge is made. This will let you know if someone has stolen your credit card information and has made unauthorized purchases.

balance!

- Credit card debt can prevent you from getting loans for much more important things like cars or homes. Two key factors considered when a lender is deciding to give you a car loan or a home mortgage loan are how much other debt you have and the amount of the monthly payments. For these reasons, keeping your credit card debt under control is important for your financial future.

- Some potential employers will run a credit report on you when doing a background check. High levels of credit card debt can reflect poorly on you as a potential employee for some types of jobs, especially jobs that require high security clearances.

- Many people, me included (in the past), have accumulated a lot of credit card debt. It happens a little bit at a time, and before you know it, you are drowning in debt. This dad's strong suggestion is that you avoid using credit cards entirely, if possible.

A credit card, if used responsibly, can be a useful tool.

- As mentioned above in the checking account section, a credit card can sometimes be used as an overdraft safety net. You attach the credit card to a checking account as your preferred method of overdraft funding to avoid or reduce overdraft fees.

- Many people also use rewards credit cards to accumulate travel miles or cashback rewards to save money or to get points for vacations. Again, if used responsibly, this can be okay.

- Using a credit card wisely can help you establish a credit history with the credit bureaus, which you will likely need at some point (see Credit History and Credit Scores below).

If you must have a credit card, shop wisely and follow these guidelines:

- Look for cards with low or no annual fee.

- Look for cards with lower interest rates than their competitors' rates.

- Many credit card companies offer 0% interest on purchases for one or more years. Use this to your advantage, but be careful. If you don't pay off the balance within the promotional period, interest will accrue on the outstanding balance at the regular rate which is usually very high.

- Then, make up your mind that you will pay off the balance every month. This is really the only way you will keep your credit card usage under control.

Credit History and Credit Scores - A major argument for using credit cards is they help you establish a credit history and a credit score. This argument has merit, but only if you use your credit cards wisely. Let me explain:

- A potential lender for loans like car and home loans, decides whether they will grant you a loan based on your credit history and credit score. Credit history is an accumulation of all the times you used credit. So, if you never used credit, you have no credit history.

- If you used credit, like with a credit card, a car loan, etc., the way you used (or abused) those credit opportunities are reported to three credit bureaus: Experian, TransUnion, and Equifax. Using a formula, these credit bureaus calculate a credit score that lenders use to grade your credit worthiness.

- Think of your credit score like your GPA in High School. That numeric score is an accumulation of your work in HS that colleges use to assess whether you are worthy of attending at their institutions. If they choose to look at a more detailed account of your work in HS, they can look at your transcript to see if you were better at some subjects than others.

- Your credit score is like your credit GPA. It allows potential creditors to look at a single number to get a high-level feel for how responsibly you used credit in the past. Then, if they choose to, they can pull your credit report (like a transcript) to see the details of why your score is what it is.

Several things go into calculating your credit score, positively or negatively:

- On-time payments – this should be obvious, but creditors value being paid on-time above most other factors. Paying your monthly payments within the payment date terms shows creditors that you are responsible.

- Credit Utilization – this is the ratio of how much credit you have outstanding vs. how much credit you have available to use. For example, if you have three credit cards with $10,000, $5,000, and $3,000 credit limits, your total credit availability is $18,000. Your outstanding balances on the three cards add up to $15,000, so your credit utilization is 83.3% ($15,000 / $18,000), which is high. A lender would see this as a negative because it may indicate you are not using your credit wisely. A high credit utilization will impact your credit score negatively. Keeping your credit utilization below 30% is the goal.

- Credit Age – this is the part of the credit score based on how long you have been using credit. If you've only had your first credit card for six months and have made your payments on time, that's great. But someone who has been using credit for 20 years has much more history with which to judge how responsible they used it. You can't control how long you've been using credit, but by exercising responsibility with your monthly payments, and keeping your overall utilization low, your credit age will take care of itself. Credit age alone, without good credit history and utilization, is useless.

While credit cards are one way to help you establish a credit history, they are not the only way. Following are a few suggestions on how you can establish credit either instead of, or in addition to, using credit cards:

- You may be able to get credit for paying your utilities, and other monthly services. Experian Boost™ is a free feature that lets you add your on-time phone, internet, cable, utility (gas, electricity, water) and some streaming payments like Netflix®, HBO™, Hulu™ and Disney+™ to your Experian credit report.

- Take out a credit builder loan - A credit builder loan is an installment loan with fixed monthly payments, like a personal loan, auto loan, and mortgage. But unlike a typical loan that allows you access to cash when you take out the loan, with a credit builder loan, your lender deposits the amount of the credit builder loan into a savings or CD account that you won't be able to access until you pay off your loan. Your on-time payments are reported to the credit bureaus and can help you establish a credit score.

- Pay installment loans on time – if you already have an installment loan, such as a car loan, be sure to make your payments on time.

- You may want to use a service like Rental Kharma or Rent Reporters that reports your rental payments to the credit bureaus. These services typically require verification with your landlord and charge a registration and monthly fee. Check with your landlord before you sign up to see if they already report your payments to the credit bureaus. This can help you save money, while potentially raising your credit score.

- After having at least one account open and on your credit report for six months, you will get a FICO Score, making your purchasing history visible to potential lenders. Your credit score will only get better the longer you maintain a positive payment history and manage your credit accounts responsibly.

- Credit scores range from 300 – 850 with the higher scores being better than lower scores. While different credit bureaus use slightly different scales, in general, a score above 700 is considered good to excellent. Scores between 650 and 699 are considered fair. 550 to 649 are considered poor. Scores below 550 are bad.

6 STUDENT LOANS

Since we were just talking about debt in the form of credit cards, this might be a good place to discuss student loans. The topic of getting student loans is important, but because this guide is primarily addressed to people starting their life on their own, I'm going to only talk about how to manage the payment of student loans that you may already have.

For many, your parent or guardian did all the heavy lifting to get your student loans set up for you. But now that you are an adult, you may be responsible for paying off at least some of these student loans. For most student loan types, you have six months from your college graduation before you must start making payments. This gives you time to get settled and financially set up. Here are a few tips on how to get a handle on your student loans:

Tip: Talk to your student loan servicer to explore all your payment options. There may be possibilities you haven't thought of. Also, explore refinancing options with other servicers. You may be able find a better rate.

- First, talk to the person who helped you get your student loans. They can probably provide you with usernames and passwords for your accounts. This will give you a good head start.

- Next, get your own account on studentaid.gov. This is a government website where you can:
    - Review your student loan balance on your dashboard.
    - Choose a repayment plan based on your income. Loan Simulator can help you decide which plan is right for you.

- Then,
    - Visit your loan servicer's website if you need help. Loan servicers are an important resource.
    - Pay your student loans online through your loan servicer's website. Tip: Set up auto pay to ensure on-time payments.
    - Review the various loan forgiveness options.

- As the last tip indicates, you may be able to get your student loan debt forgiven, meaning, getting your debt wiped away. Categories of jobs that may qualify you for loan forgiveness are:

    - Teachers
    - Government Employees
    - Non-profits
    - Nurse, Doctor, or Medical Professional
    - Those with a disability
    - Those who repay their loans through an Income-Driven Repayment Plan

- If your job sounds like any of these, you should dig deeper to see if you qualify and apply for loan forgiveness.

- If you decide to return to school and need additional student loans, the studentaid.gov site is the place to start. It will guide you through the FAFSA application process that determines your qualified types and amounts of student aid.

- Finally, if you are having trouble repaying your loans, you may consider requesting a loan deferment or forbearance:

    - With a loan deferment, you can temporarily stop making payments.
    - With a loan forbearance, you can stop making payments or reduce your monthly payments for up to 12 months.

- Because loan interest can accrue (build up) while your loan is in deferment or forbearance, you may want to explore other repayment plans first. For example, your monthly payments may be more affordable if you change to an Income-Driven Repayment Plan.

- Contact your loan servicer to discuss which path forward is best for you.

7 IDENTITY THEFT

Having just covered the major financial items, this seems like a good place to talk about identity theft. By now, most everyone knows and understands what identity theft is, but far too many tend to think, "It'll never happen to me." Unfortunately, statistics indicate that one in three U.S. citizens have been victims of identity theft at some level and the rate of these incidents is increasing at an alarming rate. Over the past 20 years, incidents of identity theft increased by 584 percent, so your odds of being a victim at some point in your lifetime are high.

Tip: Get a purse or wallet with "RFID" protection. This will stop thieves from scanning your credit cards to steal your credit card data. This is one of the most common identity theft methods.

Like roadside assistance, many sources are available for identity theft monitoring and protection. Some good places to look are with your bank or your auto insurance provider. They may have plans that are inexpensive because you are already their customer.

The three credit reporting companies, Experian, Equifax, and TransUnion, offer free credit report monitoring. Many credit monitoring services that are advertised as "free" can be found with a simple online search.

In addition to using a credit monitoring service, look at your credit report yourself at least once a year. If you see anything on it that you don't recognize, i.e., charges you didn't make, you may need to address it.

Look carefully at all these free services to be sure they provide the services you need. Credit monitoring is only half of the solution; credit protection is also important if you do become a victim. Credit protection services cover you against losses as well as the assistance necessary to repair your damaged credit.

8 AUTOMOBILES

Next to your home (whether you rent or own), your largest expense is usually your automobile. Making wise decisions regarding whether to buy a vehicle new or used, how to maintain your vehicle, as well as acquiring insurance, tags, and inspections, can be a lot to navigate when you are just getting out on your own. The following information is intended to help you understand each item a little better, but this is not intended to be exhaustive. You should consult a trusted guide such as a parent or guardian who can help you with some of the more specific details not covered in this guide.

8.1 PURCHASING A VEHICLE

Purchasing a vehicle, whether new or used, from a dealer or from an individual, is filled with potential problems. Unfortunately, many people are ready and willing to take advantage of you, especially if you are inexperienced in the car buying process.

Not every person or car dealer is dishonest, but unless you know the seller, you have no way of knowing whether they are honest or not. Therefore, rather than trying to teach you how to buy a car on your own, which is impractical in a guide of this kind, I'm just going to give you some advice: **find someone you trust who has experience purchasing cars to help you. This can be a parent or guardian, or someone from your church or your workplace, but get help.**

8.2 Auto Insurance

Auto insurance is a legal requirement in the U.S. Failure to have at least the legal minimum auto insurance can result in fines, legal fees, and even imprisonment. Consult an insurance agent to understand your state's legal minimums. You can locate a local insurance agent by looking them up online or asking someone you trust for a referral.

The legal minimum insurance is referred to as liability insurance because it protects you against being sued if you are in an accident where someone else is injured or killed. It also protects the other party in an accident, if you are at fault, by covering damage on their vehicle and medical bills, if injured.

However, depending on the type of automobile you have, the legal minimums may not be adequate. Depending on the value of your vehicle you may want to carry coverage that will replace it if it is destroyed in a traffic accident, flood, fire, or other catastrophic event.

Collision coverage pays for damage resulting from moving accidents such as colliding with another moving vehicle, or colliding with a parked car, a tree, or any other object. Collision coverage will also cover repairable damage due to fender benders.

Tip: Be careful not to over-insure your vehicle. If your car is only worth $3,000, it may not make sense to carry collision and comprehensive coverages, as this only increases your monthly premiums for little return.

In addition to moving accidents, you may also want to cover non-moving causes of damage to your vehicle. This type of coverage is referred to as comprehensive insurance. Comprehensive insurance covers damage resulting from non-moving accidents such as a tree limb falling on the car, hail damage, vandalism, etc.

Each insurance type on your automobile policy will carry its own deductible. A deductible is an amount you will pay for each event before the insurance company pays the rest. The higher the deductible, the lower your premium will be for that coverage.

"Premium" is a fancy insurance word for the amount you pay for the coverage. The best way to control your total premium is with higher deductibles. For example, say you want a low deductible such as $100 per event for collision coverage. If you are in a fender bender that is going to cost $1,500 to get repaired, you will pay $100 and the insurance company will pay $1,400. This sounds great, but it comes with a cost. Because you are accepting a small amount of the risk (cost) associated with each accident, the insurance company must charge you more for that coverage.

For example, let's assume it will cost $300/month for that $100 deductible. If you decide to accept a deductible of $1,000 per event instead, your premiums could easily drop from $300/month to $150/month. That's a difference of $1,800/year in premiums. So, even if you had an accident, and paid the $1000 deductible, you would still be $800 ahead. These are just example numbers of how insurance and deductibles work, which also illustrate the financial calculations you may need to find the best coverage for you.

Finally, you are required to carry proof of insurance with you in your vehicle. Most insurance companies provide their customers with paper insurance cards each time their policy renews. A good practice is to keep this card in your glove box with your registration card. Most insurance companies also have a smartphone app that will have an image of your insurance card as well. Digital insurance cards are accepted in 49 states and the District of Columbia. As of 2024 when this guide is being written, only in New Mexico are digital cards not explicitly accepted.

8.3 AUTO TAGS, REGISTRATION, AND TITLES

Every state in the U.S. requires you to title and register your vehicle if you become a legal resident in that state.

Tip: Familiarize yourself with the security features of car titles in your state before buying from an individual. This will help you to recognize a fake title. If possible, meet the seller at a local DMV office for title transfer.

A title is a physical legal document that proves who owns an automobile. Because of the importance of this document, an auto title usually has many security measures to make them difficult to duplicate such as watermarks, raised seals, and even holographic images like on your driver's license. The ink on titles will be in multiple colors, never only black and white, and many title documents will display a readable warning if they are copied on a copier like "NOT VALID."

Registration is a document you receive with your physical tag (license plate) from the state who issued the tag. This registration document should be kept in your vehicle. If you are stopped by a law enforcement officer, they will ask you for your driver's license and registration. Failure to produce this document could result in a ticket and fine.

When you purchase a new or used vehicle from a dealer, they will typically do the necessary paperwork for you to apply for your tag and title for the vehicle in that state. So, in these situations, you may not need to do anything to receive your tag and registration. The dealer representative should be able to instruct you on any steps you need to follow.

If you purchase a vehicle from an individual, for example through Craigslist, Facebook Marketplace, or from a friend or family member, you will need to apply for a new tag and title yourself. In these person-to-person transactions, always get the title from the seller (owner) before you pay for, and leave with, the vehicle. If you want to be sure the title is authentic and the seller is authorized to sell the vehicle, have them meet you at a local Department of Motor Vehicles (DMV) office to have the title transferred to you.

Before making the purchase transaction, go online and review the title transfer requirements and procedures for a person-to-person auto sale in your state. You should be able to see examples of exactly where the seller needs to sign the original title on back and which fields they need to complete. While the signing instructions are written on the back of the title, it can be confusing if this is your first time, so familiarizing yourself ahead of time will help to avoid costly mistakes and delays.

In addition to getting the signed title from the seller, look at the front of the title to be sure no lienholders are listed. A lien is an encumbrance associated with the title that would limit the seller's ability to sell the vehicle until the lien is removed. With automobiles, a lien is always a loan on the vehicle that has not yet been paid off. Therefore, a lienholder is the person, bank, or credit company who made the loan for the purchase of the vehicle. Until that loan is paid, the current owner cannot (legally) sell the vehicle. If you purchase the vehicle while there is still a lien on the vehicle, you will become liable for the payment of the loan before you can get a clear (no loan) title. In most cases, the lienholder holds the original title until the loan is paid off. Once the loan is paid, the lien is removed, and the clear title is sent to the owner. Therefore, in most cases, if the seller has an original title, the title is likely clear.

To apply for your tag and title, go to your nearest state or county tag office. They will assist you with the application process which will include both your tag and getting the title reissued in your name. Taxes and fees will apply based on the value of your vehicle. Just do an internet search on "getting a car tag in (your state)" to find a location near you.

A title document is an important and valuable document that represents your ownership of a vehicle. Without it, you cannot prove you own the vehicle, and if someone else steals your title, they can forge your signature and transfer ownership to themselves or someone else without your knowledge. Therefore, secure your title in a safe place such as a safe or safe deposit box just as you would other valuable documents. DO NOT CARRY YOUR TITLE IN THE GLOVE BOX OF YOUR VEHICLE! If your car is stolen, the thieves will have everything they need to take ownership and resell the car. While it might be possible to prove it was stolen through legal means and get it back, the process will be long and expensive. You can avoid the headaches by properly securing your title.

Finally, here are a few things to know about car tags:

- Tags need to be renewed each year. Most states use your birthday month as the month when your tag becomes due. Some states send out a notice in the mail a month or more before your tag is due for renewal.

- Usually, you can renew your tag online or by mail using the reminder notice by paying the necessary fees shown on the notice. Failure to renew your tag on time can result in late fees when you do renew.

- If stopped by a law enforcement officer and you have an expired tag, you may be ticketed and fined, and/or your vehicle may be impounded. Save yourself the cost and aggravation by renewing on time.

- Whenever you move to another state and take your vehicle with you, most states require that you register your vehicle in their state within 30 days of establishing residency. Consult the new state's requirements online. Go to the nearest state or county tag office to apply for your new tag. This single process will usually take care of both the tag and registration as well as retitling the vehicle in the new state.

8.4 AUTO INSPECTIONS

Many states require an annual inspection or emissions check before you can get your tag renewed. Do an online search for the tag requirements for your state and/or county before going to the tag office. If an inspection is required, you will be able to locate an inspection facility near you, as well as any applicable fees.

8.5 AUTO MAINTENANCE

Routine maintenance is important not only for the lifespan of your vehicle, but also for your personal safety. Proper care of tires, brakes, lights, etc., will keep your car safe for you and for others as well. The following items should be checked and maintained on a regular basis:

OIL CHANGES

Depending on the type of oil your vehicle uses and the manufacturer's recommendations, you should change your oil at regular intervals. If you have a newer car, it may be under warranty, so meet the minimum oil change requirements to keep your warranty intact. Consult your owner's manual or warranty documents for these guidelines.

The oil change intervals will usually be either every 3,000 or 5,000 miles. However, some full synthetic oils are rated for up to 10,000 miles between oil changes. If you are not sure, consult a trusted source such as an auto parts professional, an auto mechanic, parent, or friend for advice.

Tip: Set alarms on your phone for important car maintenance checks. Most vehicles will remind you when an oil change is due, but very few will remind you to check your tire pressure, or other important fluid levels.

"Oil types" refers to both viscosity levels and conventional vs. synthetic lubricants. While your auto parts professional will be able to provide the correct viscosity oil for your vehicle, you will have a choice between conventional, full-synthetic, and synthetic blend oils. Synthetic oils are better in many ways for your vehicle, but they are also much more expensive per quart. However, some synthetic oils can be used as much as twice as long as conventional oils so the price difference may not be as much as you think. If you can afford the higher priced synthetic, most auto professionals would recommend it. Synthetic oils are also highly recommended for older vehicles with high mileage.

You do not need to understand what all the numbers and letters on oils mean. You only need to understand that you should use the right type of oil for your vehicle. In addition to your owner's manual, any auto parts store can help you find the right oil for the year, make, and model of your vehicle.

LIGHTS

Your vehicle's lights are one of its important safety features. This is true for both nighttime and daytime driving. Mainly, be aware of headlights, taillights, and brake lights.

The importance of headlights is obvious for night driving. They help you see where you are going, and they help others see you. Headlights will fail occasionally and should be repaired as soon as possible. Not only is this true for your safety and the safety of others, but you can be ticketed by a police officer for driving without all your lights in working order. The difficulty level of changing your own headlight bulbs varies from vehicle to vehicle. Online videos can be helpful.

Taillights are the red lights on the rear of the vehicle that let other drivers see you when they are approaching from the rear. These lights are on whenever your headlights are on. Taillights on most vehicles are easy to replace yourself, but look at some online videos to make that judgement. You can also be ticketed for having a taillight out, so take care of this issue as soon as possible.

Brake lights are also on the rear of the vehicle where the taillights are, but brake lights get much brighter when you press the brake pedal. The lights get brighter to alert drivers behind you that you stopping. Most vehicles also have a third brake light in the rear window. Because of the safety importance of brake lights to avoid rearend collisions, having all three brake lights working is important. Brake lights on most vehicles are easy to replace yourself, but look at some online videos to decide. You can also be ticketed for having a brake light out, so take care of this issue as soon as possible.

Most any bulb type on your vehicle can be purchased at an auto parts store. By providing the auto parts professional with your year, make and model, they will be able to find the proper bulbs for your vehicle.

TIRES

Many modern vehicles are equipped with a Tire Pressure Monitoring System (TPMS). This is usually an image on the dashboard in the shape of a tire as shown.

This image will appear when the air pressure in the tire is below the proper level. If the TPMS alert image appears, get your tires checked right away.

In addition to the TPMS light, you should check your tire pressure on a regular basis to ensure safe and efficient performance. Tire pressure can be too high or too low without necessarily triggering the TPMS alert. Improper tire pressure may cause your tires to wear unevenly, shortening the life of your tires as well as causing them to perform poorly such as poor braking, poor handling, sliding in wet weather, or other performance issues. Low tire pressure will also reduce your gas mileage. You can purchase an inexpensive tire pressure gauge at an auto parts store or even at Walmart or other stores that sell basic auto parts and tools. An auto parts store professional can also show you how to use it. I recommend everyone have a tire pressure gauge in their glove box.

Despite performing all the tire maintenance measures above, it is still possible, even likely that sooner or later you will have a flat tire. Leaks are most often caused by foreign objects in the roadway such as nails, screws, scrap metal, etc. Therefore, everyone needs to know how to change a tire. Just because you may have a roadside assistance membership (to be discussed below), their response times may be several hours, and you may not wish to wait on them. So, I highly recommend you learn how to change a tire on your vehicle BEFORE you have an emergency. Ask someone you know to help you learn and/or watch some YouTube videos for your year, make and model. Be sure to practice it at least once to be sure you can do it. Always be sure your vehicle is on a level surface before attempting to change a tire.

BRAKES

You should get your brakes checked at least annually to be sure your rotors and pads are not excessively worn.

There is also a dashboard warning symbol for brakes as shown.

Brake pads are the part of the brake that presses against the rotors to cause your vehicle to stop. Pads are manufactured to be soft so they are designed to wear out over time.

Rotors can last for the life of a vehicle if the pads are not allowed to wear too far and damage the rotors.

Inspect your brakes annually or when you are having other routine maintenance performed to ensure your pads are still good.

WIPER BLADES

Windshield wiper blades should be inspected and replaced when they become worn. Wiper blades over time will be get dry and begin to crack. This will usually cause them to squeak and perform poorly, leaving streaks and in some cases missing sections of the windshield altogether. For your safety during rainy weather, be sure to maintain your wiper blades as needed.

Because many automobiles have different length wipers on each side of the windshield, wiper blades are sold individually, not in pairs. To determine the correct size blades for your vehicle, consult an auto parts professional who can look up your wiper blade sizes for your year, make and model of vehicle.

FLUID LEVELS

Learn how to check your vehicle's fluids yourself. You can ask your auto mechanic, a parent, or even look it up online. Many available DIY videos show you how to check fluid levels on your specific year, make, and model of vehicle.

The most common fluid levels to check in your vehicle are motor oil, power steering fluid, transmission fluid, brake fluid, engine coolant and windshield washer fluid. Of these, motor oil and engine coolant are the most important to keep an eye on and are the easiest to check yourself. Following are several dashboard lights for fluids:

- Oil Pressure Light - This usually indicates your oil level is low. Address this issue right away! You should also see this symbol on the oil fill cap in the engine compartment to show you where to add oil.

- Power Steering Fluid – If your power steering fluid is low, you should see this warning light. Usually, if your power steering fluid is low, you will hear a roaring sound when you turn the steering wheel, especially at low speeds.

- Engine Coolant – this dash light can indicate that your engine coolant (antifreeze/coolant) is low. It can also indicate your engine is overheating. This may be an urgent and serious situation. Do not ignore it! You should also see this symbol on the coolant fill cap in the engine compartment to show you where to add coolant.

- Windshield Washer Fluid – When your windshield washer fluid is low, this warning light will appear. This is not serious or urgent but should be handled eventually. The window washer fluid reservoir is usually transparent so you can see where the fluid level is just by looking at it. You should also see this symbol on the washer fluid fill cap in the engine compartment to show you where to add washer fluid.

Year, make, and model of a vehicle is the year the vehicle was manufactured, the company that manufactured the vehicle such as Ford, Chevrolet, Mercedes, and the model of the vehicle such as Impala, F-150, Corvette, respectively.

If you aren't sure of your year, make, and model, you can consult your owner's manual; it will be printed on the front cover.

Or look up the Vehicle Identification Number (VIN) online. Every vehicle manufactured in the U.S. and most other countries since 1981 have a unique (VIN). On most vehicles you can find it on a sticker on the door jamb on the driver's side. It is a 17-digit alpha-numeric number. You can do an online search for "VIN lookup" or "VIN decoder" and enter your VIN to find your year, make, and model.

Know your year, make, and model even if you don't check your own fluid levels. You will need it for title and tag applications, when you take your vehicle to an auto mechanic for maintenance or repairs, and at auto parts stores if you simply need parts.

Find your year, make, and model and write it below for future reference:

_____   _____   _____

     YEAR   MAKE   MODEL

CHECK ENGINE LIGHT

At some point in the life of your vehicle the check engine light will appear on your dash. The check engine light is an icon that looks like an engine as shown.

A check engine light is an indication that something is wrong with your engine, which can range from something harmless to something serious, so it should not be ignored.

The easiest and quickest way to determine the nature and seriousness of this alert is to take your vehicle to an auto parts store such as Advance Auto Parts, AutoZone, O'Reilly Auto Parts, tell them you have a check engine light, and ask them to run the codes for you. Any of these stores will run your codes free of charge and can at least provide you with the codes which you can look up on the internet to get some indication of the nature of the codes.

Some codes may be non-specific and can indicate one of several issues, but usually the code can narrow the field of possibilities and provide some indication of severity.

Some of these auto parts stores may even look up the codes for you and suggest a repair location if you do not have a trusted mechanic of your own.

AUTO REPAIR SHOPS

Get referrals from friends or family to find an auto mechanic if you don't already have a trusted auto shop in mind. If you are new to a location, ask your friends, co-workers, or other associates in your new community for recommendations.

If you are unable to get a referral from a trusted associate, look up auto mechanics on the internet and check their online reviews. If you are unfamiliar with how automobiles work in general, and how much repairs should cost, a dishonest auto shop might easily take advantage of you.

Tip: Many oil change locations will also check your other critical fluid levels as well as tire pressure when they change your oil. Look for quick oil change companies like Jiffy Lube, Express Oil Change, and similar companies.

Don't be afraid to get a second opinion from another auto shop on high dollar repairs.

As mentioned in the warranty section, you may need to use a dealership for warranty repairs to keep your warranty intact. However, you do not need to continue using a dealership for repairs and service once you are off warranty. If you like the dealership's service and are satisfied with their charges, there is nothing wrong with using them. Just understand that many capable mechanics can service your vehicle, often at a lower cost than at a dealership.

8.6 WARRANTIES

Auto warranties are great when they come with a new vehicle. Many routine maintenance items are covered at a dealership at no additional cost and many repairs are covered free as well. Familiarize yourself with the terms of your warranty so you don't void it by missing key maintenance milestones or using unauthorized repair shops.

On the other hand, be careful about warranties offered on used vehicles. If you are buying a car at a used car dealership, you will be offered an extended warranty. Purchasing an extended auto warranty on a used car may not be what you expect it to be. They promise far more than they ever deliver. Many extended warranties make it sound like every repair will be covered, but no warranty covers everything. Most extended warranties have an extensive exception list of the repairs they do not cover, which unsurprisingly, are many of the most expensive repair items.

I tried to not paint with too broad of a brush by indicating that every extended warranty is not worth the cost, but use caution when considering one.

8.7 ROADSIDE ASSISTANCE COVERAGE

One of the most dangerous situations you can be in when driving is being stranded on the roadside. A flat tire, running out of gas, or a mechanical breakdown can occur no matter how diligent you are with the auto maintenance items above. Get help quickly.

Everyone should have some sort of roadside assistance coverage. Roadside assistance provides you with a single telephone number to call 24/7/365 that can get help you almost anywhere in the U.S. The primary service they provide is towing service. In most cases, they will dispatch a tow truck to your location to tow your vehicle to a repair shop or to your home, if required. Most roadside breakdowns will result in a tow. While you might be able to call a tow truck yourself, the roadside service providers have access to a nationwide network and will likely get service to you much quicker.

Besides tow truck services, most roadside assistance companies also provide lockout services if you lock yourself out of your car, gas service if you run out of gas, jump-starting service if your car won't start, and other services.

You can subscribe to different levels of service with any roadside assistance company, but the services within your package will be covered at no additional change. If you are worried about the cost of a roadside assistance package, consider this; the cost of one tow would often be more than your annual cost for a plan.

However, you can get roadside assistance in other ways without subscribing with a major company like AAA. Many (if not most) auto insurance companies offer roadside assistance plans as an add-on to your auto insurance inexpensively. Some even offer free plans to persuade you to sign up with their company. Check with your auto insurance agent or customer service. Also, some cell phone plans offer inexpensive plans that you can add to your monthly phone bill. In the end, you should be able to afford some level of roadside assistance plan.

Tip: Even if you have a roadside assistance membership, you should still learn how to change a tire. Response times for roadside assistance companies can be as long as four hours depending on how busy they are.

Even if you have a roadside assistance plan, always have a few items in your vehicle, like jumper cables, flares, a poncho, reflective triangles, and a flashlight. Roadside safety kits can be purchased from Amazon, Walmart, auto parts stores, and many other places and will include all the safety items you need in a single package.

8.8 AUTO ACCIDENT PROCEDURES

Having just discussed roadside assistance for breakdown situations, this is a good place to discuss what to do in the event of an auto accident. Whether you have a collision with another vehicle or a single vehicle accident, you will need to know the right things to do. Even experienced drivers often make critical errors under the stress of the moment, so have these steps printed out in your glove box, or readily accessible on your smart phone:

- BE SAFE! If possible, before doing anything else, get yourself to a safe position. If you are able, move away from the roadway traffic and the damaged vehicles.
- Call 9-1-1 - Whether you are in a single- or multi-vehicle accident, this will get the police to the scene as quickly as possible. You may need a police report later for either insurance purposes, a legal case, or both. If anyone is injured, let the 9-1-1 operator know so they can dispatch medical assistance.

- If possible, call a parent, guardian, or friend who lives in the area. They may be able to come to the scene for support, advice, or a ride.

- Don't argue with the other driver – this won't help anyone and can only escalate the situation.

- Get any witnesses' names and contact information. Witnesses may not hang around until the police arrive and the police could miss talking to every witness.

- If possible, and safe to do so, take pictures of both vehicles and the accident scene. These may come in handy later for either insurance purposes and/or legal action. Many auto insurance smart phone apps now provide the ability to upload accident pictures directly from your smart phone.

- If possible, take pictures of the front and back of the other driver's insurance card.

- Treat everyone with respect, especially the police officer.

- Gather your valuables from the vehicle if it needs to be towed or if you are leaving in an ambulance. You may not see the car again for a while.

8.9 DRIVER'S LICENSES

You probably already have a driver's license, so I won't talk about how to get your first one here. However, all states require that you renew your driver's license every few years, keep your address information current, and that you get a valid license in their state when becoming a resident there.

Tip: Set up a reminder on your phone for several months before your driver's license expiration date. This will give you adequate time to take care of any requirements for getting your license renewed before the expiration date.

All states require you to report a change of address within a certain number of days after your move. Look up the requirements for your state and make the address changes accordingly. Address changes can be made online and you can receive your new driver's license by mail. Typically, a small fee for the new license applies.

If you lose your driver's license, you can get a replacement in most states either online, or at a driver's license office. There is usually a small fee for a replacement license.

If you already own a car, of course you already have a driver's license. However, when you move to another state within the U.S., you are required to get a valid driver's license in that state. Do an internet search for, "getting a driver's license in the state of _____," to get both the requirements, as well as locations near you for getting the new license.

Most states have reciprocity agreements with most other states which allow you to receive a license in their state if you already have a valid license from another state. When this is the case, you usually will not be required to take either a written or driving test for your new state's license. Check the new state's requirements for specific details.

Most states require you to get the new license within 30 days of establishing residency in their state. If you are stopped by a law enforcement officer, you could be ticketed and fined for failure to meet the requirements for a new license.

9 HEALTH INSURANCE

Be aware of health insurance when you start adulting. If you live at home and/or are supported by a parent or guardian, you have probably been covered by their health insurance up to this point. Therefore, you may have no knowledge of how health insurance works, whether you need it or not, or where to get it. So, pay special attention to this section to be sure you are adequately covered.

Depending on your age when you first leave home to live on your own, you may be able to continue under your parent's or guardian's health insurance policy. At the time of writing this guide, legal dependents may continue under their parent's or guardian's health insurance until their 26th birthday. If you are under 26 years old, be sure to check with your parent or guardian to be sure your coverage is intact and that their intention is to allow you to remain on their policy until age 26.

Tip: Be sure you always have health insurance coverage. Not only is it now a legal requirement for all U.S. citizens, but you can jeopardize not only your own, but also your loved ones' financial futures.

If you are already past your 26th birthday or are unable to remain on the policy of your parent or guardian, you need to arrange for your own health insurance coverage. As of January 1, 2014, in the U.S., you must have at least minimum health insurance coverage. Failure to do so can result in monetary penalties when you file your tax return for the calendar year (tax returns to be discussed below).

However, not only is it a legal requirement, not having adequate coverage in the event of a serious accident or illness places you and your family members in financial jeopardy. Medical costs can accumulate to hundreds of thousands of dollars in a short time if you are hospitalized for even a few days. Without adequate health insurance, you and your family members may be liable for a large medical bill which could be financially ruining to you and them. **You never know when a catastrophic accident or illness may occur, so you should be diligent to ensure you always have some level of coverage.**

So where do you go to find health insurance coverage? Here are three possible sources in order of preferability:

1. Employer-provided plans – If you are employed full-time, and your employer has at least 50 full-time employees, they are required to offer some level of health insurance coverage. Employer-provided plans are usually your best option for two reasons:
    a) the cost is usually lower than individual plans because the group is larger. When all the employees of a large company are grouped together on a particular plan, the overall premiums are lower for everyone in the group, and
    b) many employers pay a portion of your premiums for you, reducing the amount you pay. In many cases, you must work for the company for a specified number of days, e.g. 30, 60, 90 days before qualifying for your employer's plan. This is called a "probationary period." Ask your benefits specialist at your workplace for details.

If you find yourself without health insurance during this probationary period, you may be able to get a short-term policy through an independent insurance agent (see option 3 below).

2. HealthCare.gov is a U.S. Government sponsored marketplace for individuals seeking healthcare coverage. The plans offered there are specific to the state you live in. Most of these plans have high deductibles (the amount you must pay before the insurance starts paying) but depending on your income level, you may be eligible for a tax credit to offset part of the premiums. The tax credits are subtracted from your monthly premiums. If you underreport your income, or your income increases during the year causing your available tax credit to be reduced, this will be reconciled when you file your tax return at the end of the year.

3. Independent insurance agent – ask a trusted associate for a referral for an insurance agent who can help you locate a health insurance policy to meet your needs. Many insurance agents specialize in particular types of insurance such as home, auto, or life insurance, so not just any insurance agent will necessarily provide health insurance. However, they can likely refer you to an agent who does. This will probably be the most expensive option of the three provided here, so be sure to exhaust options 1 and 2 above first.

10 LIFE INSURANCE

As the name indicates, life insurance insures your life. If you have life insurance when you die, the life insurance company pays a death benefit to your beneficiaries. The short answer for young adults with no dependents is, you don't need life insurance. If that is all you want to know about life insurance right now, skip to the next section. If you want to know more, read on.

Most financial advisors agree that life insurance is not necessary, or even advised, for young, single adults. Life insurance is primarily for the purpose of replacing your income for your family in the event of your untimely death. Whether you are married or have children will determine whether you need life insurance or not, and if so, how much. If you are married and/or have children who cannot support themselves without all or part of your income, life insurance may be needed.

The two main types of life insurance are whole life and term life insurance. Without going into the differences in detail, the name "whole life" means the policy is in force for your whole life if you continue to pay your premiums. Whole life insurance is more expensive because it has both an insurance element and a savings element as part of your premium.

Term life insurance, on the other hand, is for a specific term (number of years). For example, you may purchase a ten-year term life policy, so the term is ten years. At the end of ten years, that policy expires and you may sign up for a new policy if you wish. The monthly or annual premiums for term life policies are much less than those of whole life policies because the premium is only for insurance, not for a savings component. Because the term of the policy is limited, the risk to the insurer (the insurance company behind the policy) is far less than a policy covering your whole life.

While opinions are mixed on the relative merits of whole life and term life policies, within the context of this guide that is directed to younger adults, term life will be your best choice if you think you need life insurance at all.

If you have health insurance through your employer, in many cases, the same insurer offering your health insurance will also offer inexpensive life insurance. Employer plans for life insurance are your least expensive option by far since they are offered for pennies on the dollar compared to other plans.

In any case, term life insurance for a young adult will be inexpensive. If you determine that you need life insurance based on the criteria discussed above, consult a trusted agent who can help you decide on an adequate amount.

11 WORKPLACE BENEFITS

I f you are starting your first job with a company that offers a comprehensive benefits package, you may find yourself swimming in unfamiliar waters. This section familiarizes you with many of the most common employer benefit offerings so you can start with at least some level of understanding.

11.1 HEALTH INSURANCE
(SEE THE HEALTH INSURANCE SECTION ABOVE FOR DETAILS)

11.2 Life Insurance
(SEE THE LIFE INSURANCE SECTION ABOVE FOR DETAILS)

11.3 401(K)

Perhaps you've heard of a 401(k) but have no idea what it is and what to do with it. This section will give you the basic information you need to understand whether you want to participate in one. Because of its relative importance to you and your family's future, I will spend more time discussing this topic than many other topics in this guide.

So to answer, "Should I participate in my company's 401(k)?", the answer, in my opinion, is always a resounding, "YES!" But before I tell you why my answer is always, "yes," first let me explain what a 401(k) is.

> Tip: Start contributing to your company's 401(k) plan as early as you can. When it comes to investing, time is your ally. If you don't have much income to spare, start small and gradually add more each year.

A 401(k) is an employer sponsored, tax-advantaged, retirement savings plan, named for the subsection of the U.S. Internal Revenue Service code where it is found.

Most companies of any size offer a 401(k) plan to their employees. Usually after a probationary period which varies from company to company, you will be offered the opportunity to contribute a percentage of your gross pay to the company's 401(k) plan.

THE TIME VALUE OF MONEY

Before I go further, I need to interject something important here in this discussion on 401(k)s; "the time value of money."

If all I did in this guide was to describe what 401(k)s, IRAs, SEPs, and Roth IRAs are, without explaining why they are so valuable, you might not see the point. If all you are doing is putting money into a savings account, then why not do that in a bank account, a piggy bank, or in your mattress? The answer is, "the time value of money." Let me give you an example:

- *If you started saving $50 every month in a piggy bank when you turn 25 and continued until you turn 65, on your 65th birthday you would have $24,000.*

- *If you started saving $50 every month from age 25 to 65 in an investment account that yields an average of 6% per year return, on your 65th birthday you would have $99,574.54.*

- *Because you saved a small but consistent amount, over a long period of time, while receiving a modest return on your investment, the savings had a snowball effect. For example, below are the savings balances after 10, 20, 30 and 40 years using the same example:*

  - *After 10 years = $8,193.97*
  - *After 20 years = $23,102.04*
  - *After 30 years = $50,225.75*
  - *After 40 years = $99,574.54*

- *As you can see, the growth of the account gained momentum as the years passed, and in fact, doubled in the last 10 years alone. This is referred to as, "the time value of money."*

- *Why is this important to someone just getting started in their career when retirement is so far in the future? Because the earlier you start, the bigger your savings will grow, without changing the amount you save. If you wait until later to start saving, you can never get the lost time back. Like the example above shows, if you started saving just 10 years later, but still saved $50/month for 30 years at 6% return, your ending balance would be half the amount.*

Now, back to the discussion of 401(k)s.

As I was saying, usually after a probationary period which varies from company to company, you will be offered the opportunity to contribute a percentage of your gross pay to the company's 401(k) plan with <u>pre-tax</u> dollars and in most cases your employer will match a portion of your contribution up to a set percentage of your gross pay.

The term "pre-tax" means before the dollars are taxed, so when you can contribute pre-tax money, those dollars are not reported on your tax return for the year in which they were earned, so you don't have to pay tax on that portion of your income in the current year. When the funds are withdrawn in retirement, they will be taxable, so the most accurate term here is "tax-deferred" since the taxes are being deferred until later. Now, with this basic information in front of you, let me provide a simple example so you can get your head around the numbers and the reason for my emphatic "YES!" above:

- Let's say your annual salary in your new job is $50,000. Your company's 401(k) plan matches your contributions up to 3% of your annual salary.

- You decide to contribute 5% of your gross salary to the 401(k) so your annual contribution will be $50,000 X 0.05 = $2,500 per year.

- Your employer will match up to 3% of your salary, and since you are contributing 5%, you are maximizing the company match. $50,000 x 0.03 = $1,500 of FREE MONEY!

- At the end of year one, you will have $4,000 ($2,500 + $1,500) not including any investment gains (or losses).

- So you invested $2,500 and got an automatic $1,500 return which is a 60% return on investment (ROI). A better investment on the planet does not exist where you can receive a 60% ROI, GUARANTEED!

- Remember that your contributions are pre-tax, which means you don't have to pay taxes on that portion ($2,500) of your income until retirement. So, when you receive your W-2 (W-2s will be discussed in the tax return section below) at the end of the year, instead of reporting the full $50,000 of your salary, only $47,500 will be reported as taxable income ($50,000 -$2,500).

- If your tax rate is 20% when everything is considered on your tax return, since you contributed $2,500 of pre-tax money, you will save $500 on your tax return ($2,500 x 0.20 = $500). When you add that $500 to the $1,500 of employer match, now your ROI for the year is $2,000, which is an 80% ROI.

Going back to the time value of money:

In addition to the ROI bonus you are getting from your company's match, and the tax savings you are receiving, we need to consider the effect of this same scenario over 40 years, contributing just 5% of your salary each year (a conservative amount), receiving a 3% company match, getting a conservative 2% annual salary increase, and yielding an average of 6% return on your investments:

- *Your total contributions for the 40 years would be $151,004.96*

- *Your company's match would be $90,602.97*

- *Your total balance in the investment account at age 65 would be -*

$867,516.65

I HOPE YOUR MIND IS SUFFICIENTLY BLOWN!

In this example, if you waited just 10 years to start saving at the same rate (30 years), your balance at 65 would only be $499,008.19 - a difference of $368,508.50 just for waiting.

TIME IS YOUR ALLY WHEN SAVING AND INVESTING.

DON'T WASTE IT; YOU CAN NEVER GET IT BACK.

Now, despite this compelling financial illustration, many (perhaps most) young adults do not choose to participate in their company's 401(k) for several reasons:

- They don't think they can afford to make the contributions because they think they need to live on those dollars. In some cases this is true, but in most cases if you look hard enough at your budget, you can find room for at least a 1% contribution.

- They don't understand how 401(k)s work. This no longer applies to you because I've just explained them to you.

- They don't trust the company with their money. All 401(k) plans are federally regulated and insured, so companies are not free to use those funds for purposes that put them at risk, at least not legally.

If you fall into reason 1 above, a good strategy is to start small and gradually work your way up as your pay increases year to year. Start with 1% in the first year with a plan to increase it by 1% each subsequent year. Even if you only receive cost of living raises most years, those raises will likely be between 2 and 3% per year, so by increasing your 401(k) contributions by 1%, you will still have a net gain to your discretionary income (the amount left over after you pay all your monthly bills).

Finally, once you begin to contribute funds to the 401(k) plan, you can then choose from a group of investment vehicles offered within your company's plan. Investments will typically range from conservative (low risk and lower returns) to aggressive (high risk and potentially higher returns) depending on your personal investment goals and willingness to accept risk. If you don't know how to invest, your company may be able to assist you.

11.4 FLEXIBLE SPENDING ACCOUNT

A flexible spending account (FSA) is a company-sponsored savings plan that you can use during the same calendar year for medical and medical-related expenses. Like the 401(k) plan, participation is optional. First, let me cover the basics.

Each calendar year, you are given the opportunity to decide if, and how much to contribute from each paycheck toward your FSA plan. Like the 401(k), dollars contributed to your company's FSA plan are pre-tax dollars (see 401(k) section for a discussion of pre-tax dollars). Once these funds are contributed, you may use them for any out-of-pocket medical expenses that your health insurance does not cover. Expenses may include doctor visit co-pays, prescriptions drugs, dental visits, and even over-the-counter drugs such as Tylenol, Pepto-Bismol, etc.

> Tip: Flexible Spending Accounts provide free money for out-of-pocket medical expenses, but many employees throw this benefit in the trash. Even if you start with a small amount, get used to using this very valuable benefit.

Because your contributions are pre-tax, you don't have to pay taxes on those dollars, ever. So let's do another financial example with some numbers:

- Say you expect to spend at least $1000 during the year on medical related expenses for you and members of your family, so you sign up to have $1,000 deducted from your pay in equal amounts based on your pay frequency. For example, if you are paid monthly, your company would deduct 1/12 of $1,000 or $83.33 per month. After three months, you have $250 in your FSA account.

- In March, you need to go to the doctor, and after your health insurance pays its part, you pay $100 out-of-pocket. You then receive $100 of reimbursement from your FSA plan. Those are the simple mechanics of how an FSA plan works, but if that was all there was to it, what would be the point of putting money into an account just to take it out later?

- Well, don't forget that the $1000 is pre-tax. So, when you get your W-2 at the end of the year, your gross taxable amount will be reduced by $1000. Assuming the same 20% tax rate as before, you saved $200 on your tax return, so in effect, you only paid $800 for $1000 of medical and medical related expenses. It's like having a 20% discount coupon for all your out-of-pocket medical costs.

Again, the unfortunate truth is most employees do not avail themselves of their company's FSA plan for the same reasons they don't participate in their 401(k) plan, and the biggest of those reasons is they don't understand how they work.

But as you can see from the example above, not participating in a free FSA plan is the same as if you had that 20% OFF coupon in your pocket, and you tossed it in the garbage because you would rather pay full price. Not very smart, right?

One last thing about FSA plans. At the beginning of each year, you are required to estimate how much you will spend in out-of-pocket medical costs. The goal is to estimate those costs as closely as possible to what you will actually spend. Some FSA plans have a "use it or lose it" policy, so you run the risk of losing any unused funds left over at the end of the year. So, it is better to underestimate than overestimate. FSA plan rules vary from company to company, so check your company's rules before you decide how much to contribute. In recent years, many FSA plans have done away with the "use it or lose it" rules and allow participants to carryover unused funds to the next calendar year. Check with your company's benefits specialist for your plan's rules.

11.5 SHORT-TERM DISABILITY

Short-term disability insurance is an insurance that covers lost wages due to a medical emergency. Your company will pay the premiums for this coverage, or you may pay the premiums yourself. Premiums for this coverage are typically inexpensive and if you pay the premiums yourself, any benefit payments will be non-taxable.

Most short-term disability plans have a coverage period of three to six months. Plan rules will vary, so check the details of your company's plan before deciding.

Whether you decide to accept coverage or not is up to you, but because of the relatively low cost, having this type of coverage is worth it just in case something unexpected happens that keeps you from working.

11.6 SELF-EMPLOYED BENEFITS ALTERNATIVES

If you are self-employed, that is, you are a small business owner, or are working as an independent contractor, you will need to provide your own benefits. The following are some alternative options for self-employed people:

SIMPLIFIED EMPLOYEE PENSION PLAN (SEP)

A SEP is roughly equivalent to a 401(k) plan for self-employed people to save for retirement with pre-tax dollars. They receive some of the same benefits as employed people. SEPs have some of the same rules as 401(k)s, but some rules are different. If you are starting your own business and want to know more about SEPs, contact a financial planning professional.

INDIVIDUAL RETIREMENT ACCOUNT (IRA)

IRAs are available to any taxpayer in the U.S. Contributions to an IRA can be deducted from your taxable income up to an annual limit defined by the U.S. government. Even taxpayers participating in their company's 401(k) plan can also use IRAs as another part of their retirement savings strategy.

IRA contributions can be paid through April 15th of the year following a tax year, but may be deducted from taxable income for the prior year. Therefore, if you finished preparing your tax return prior to April 15th and find that you owe taxes, and if you have the liquid funds available, you can contribute them into an IRA and reduce your taxable income for the prior tax year, reducing your tax liability for that prior year. As mentioned above, annual limits apply to the amount you may contribute to IRAs for tax deferral purposes. Consult a financial advisor or tax professional for details.

ROTH IRA

Another type of IRA is called a Roth IRA, named after Sen. William Roth who led the charge to create this unique retirement plan. Unlike the standard IRA discussed above, contributions to a Roth IRA are made post-tax. Post-tax means you already paid taxes on the money you will contribute to the Roth. While this will not garner you the tax benefit of deferring taxes on those contributions in the current tax year, unlike the 401(k) and standard IRA, all the growth that occurs on your Roth funds is tax-free even when you withdraw those funds in retirement.

By "growth," I mean, that portion of the account resulting from investment gains. Over a lifetime of contributing and investing, your investment gains will likely (not guaranteed) be even more than your total contributions.

HEALTH INSURANCE

(See the health insurance section above for details on getting health insurance as a self-employed individual. Options 2 and 3 only will apply to self-employed individuals unless your company has implemented its own group health insurance plan.)

12 RENTING VS. BUYING A HOME

The largest of your monthly expenses will be your living arrangements. Whether you decide to rent or buy a home, you'll need some basic information to avoid making costly mistakes. This section will equip you with some of that information.

12.1 Renting a Home

Since this guide is geared toward newly independent adults, in most cases, your first home will be rented or leased, rather than purchased. Below are a few tips about what to expect when renting your first home:

RENTAL/LEASE AGREEMENT/CONTRACT

Tip: Be careful about committing yourself to long-term lease agreements. While the monthly rent may be less, the penalties for breaking the lease can be substantial, leaving you worse off than paying a higher monthly rent.

In most rental arrangements, the owner or manager of the property will control the rental/lease agreement, so you won't have much say on the verbiage (wording) of the contract. However, you should still read the agreement before signing it to be sure it doesn't include anything unexpected you may not want to agree to. While you may not be able to persuade the owner to revise the language in the agreement, you have the option to walk away.

Reading the rental agreement is important so that you fully understand all costs such as monthly rent, rent payment due date and grace period if applicable, late fees, damage deposits, pet deposits, and other possible charges. Also, be aware of the term of the agreement (length of time you are obligated to stay in the property) and any penalties for breaking the agreement before the end of the term.

RENTER'S INSURANCE

Though not a requirement, depending on the value of your personal property such as furniture, appliances, jewelry, and electronics, you may want to get renter's insurance. Renter's insurance is relatively inexpensive and covers you against personal property loss due to theft, fire, flood, or other causes. Consult an insurance agent to assist you in finding an adequate renter's policy. Your new landlord may also be able to help you find an agent.

UTILITIES

In some rental situations, such as apartment complexes, some, or all, of your utilities may be included with your rent payment. However, this is usually the exception, so you may need to take care of setting up your own utilities. Utilities are the services you need for a home such as electricity, natural gas or propane, internet service, garbage pickup, and water.

First, ask your landlord for the names of all the utility providers. In most cases, each utility type will have one provider (for example, one electrical provider, one for water, etc.). In some cases, you may have more than one choice for natural gas or propane and garbage pickup, and your landlord will be able to help you with this information. Please note that not all homes need natural gas or propane. Only homes with at least one gas appliance such as a water heater or gas stove or range, need gas. If your landlord doesn't provide you with a gas provider, you probably don't need one.

Once you have the contact information for each utility provider, contact them to request services. You may be able to set up these services online, but you may have to call (on the phone) for others. If you are not sure what a "phone" is, it's that green button on your smartphone you use to talk to people directly. Just kidding, but I know how much most people hate using the phone, and I'm one of them.

As a first-time utilities subscriber, you may be required to pay a deposit. Utility deposits are often held by the utility provider for the duration of your service. The deposit is returned when you stop the utility upon leaving the property, or in some cases after you have established a history of on-time payments with the utility provider. In some cases, a deposit can be waived if you can get someone with established credit history to co-sign for you, such as a parent or guardian. To "co-sign" is to "sign with" someone else. A co-signer is usually someone with established credit history and/or assets who by co-signing agrees to be liable for the charges if you do not pay them.

12.2 Buying a Home

Most newly independent adults are not financially ready to purchase a home right away. However, every aspect of adulting does not occur all at once. So, this section will be here when you are ready for it.

The home buying process can be complicated and confusing if you are not familiar with it. While this section is not intended to teach you everything you need to know, you should be equipped with enough information so you know what to look for and where to look for it.

First, what are some reasons for buying instead of just renting? Though the following generalizations may not apply in every situation, home ownership is often better than renting for these reasons:

- In many cases, buying a home doesn't cost any more per month than renting.

- When you buy instead of renting you are building equity. Equity is the portion of the home's value that is yours vs. your lender's. Most homeowners must get a loan (a mortgage) from a lender to be able to purchase a home. If the fair market value of the home on a particular date is $200,000, and you owe $150,000 on your mortgage, your equity in the home is the difference of $50,000. In other words, if you sold the house today for $200,000 and paid off the mortgage of $150,000, your net from the sale would be $50,000. Though not quite that simple, for illustration purposes, we'll keep it that simple for now.

- In most economies in the U.S., good or bad, real estate (houses and land) increases in value over time. So, real estate is usually a great investment because your equity grows as the value of your home increases. This is never guaranteed, but it is generally the rule rather than the exception.

- If you own your own home, you have more control over how you use the property.

To be fair, renting also has some advantages:

- In most cases, your landlord or management company handles all repairs for you.

- Moving is faster and less trouble because you won't have to sell a home first.

- The initial costs of getting into a rental property are far less than with purchasing a home.

Tip: A major decision point for renting instead of buying a home is how long you expect to be in your current location. Buying and selling homes is expensive, so unless you expect to own a home for several years, you may need to wait.

With these general principals before you, let's dig into some of the details of buying a home:

REAL ESTATE AGENTS

When buying a home (houses or condominiums), you will need a real estate agent to help with the process. Most people ask their friends or relatives for a referral to find a trusted agent. Real estate agents can assist you with the entire buying process including searching for homes in your price range and preferred location, setting up showings of potential homes, advising, making offers to sellers, negotiating terms, and coordinating the closing process. Don't go it alone as a buyer. Since the real estate agent's commissions are paid by the seller, you aren't saving any money by not using a real estate agent.

EARNEST MONEY

When you make an offer to purchase a home, typically you are required to put up a deposit called "earnest money" with the offer, which is both a legal requirement to make the contract binding, and also a show of good faith to demonstrate to the seller that you are a serious buyer. The earnest money payment can be any amount agreed upon by the buyer and seller, but it is usually several thousand dollars with the amount being higher based on the asking price of the home.

Once an offer is accepted by the seller, the earnest money deposit can be forfeited to the seller if the buyer reneges on his agreement to purchase the home. Because the amount of the earnest money payment is usually a significant amount of money, most people are not willing to walk away and forfeit that amount of money.

DUE DILIGENCE PERIOD

Some states allow a period of due diligence during which a prospective buyer may walk away for any reason without losing their earnest money or suffering any legal action from the seller. The length of this due diligence period is stated in the original contract and can be any length of time that both parties agree to, typically between seven and fourteen days.

As the name indicates, this due diligence period provides the buyer adequate time to perform their due diligence (reasonable steps to determine the truth or value of some endeavor). As mentioned in the section below on home inspections, if you get your inspection done within this due diligence period, and some of the items on the inspection report cause you undue concern, you may walk away from the contract with no fear of reprisals or forfeiture of your earnest money deposit.

HOME INSPECTIONS

Most buyers want to have a home inspection performed prior to completing the purchase of a home. The buyer and buyer's agent should select their own inspector to ensure independence.

The home inspector performs a thorough inspection of the property to find any defects that may need to be addressed by the seller. In some states, you may have the option to back out of the contract if items found during the inspection are too serious for you to accept. I covered this in more detail in the "Due Diligence period" section above.

Once the inspection is completed, you can request that the seller make the necessary repairs before closing. However, the seller is not required to make these repairs; this is entirely negotiable. In many cases, the seller may opt to make some or all the repairs, but they may refuse to make any repairs at all. It will depend mostly on your real estate market. If the seller has been trying to sell the home for a while and is very motivated to complete the sale, they will be more likely to make the repairs. However, if homes are in short supply with several willing buyers, the seller will not be motivated to spend any time or money on repairs.

SURVEYS

A survey is a physical measurement of the boundaries of the land associated with a house to be certain that no one has any legal claim on the land due to a past mistake on a previous survey or closing document during prior sales of the same property.

Surveys are not always required in every state, but they are highly recommended for the reasons already stated. If you were to close on the property only to learn later that your property line is encroaching on another owner's property line, you could be held legally liable for the problem.

SEPTIC TANK INSPECTION

A septic system is used with homes that are too far from a city or town to connect to a city sewer system. A septic system is made up of a large underground holding tank connected to field lines which are a series of underground pipes running through the yard of the home. When sinks are drained, toilets are flushed, showers are drained, etc., the water travels into the holding tank first. Then, that water drains into the field lines and eventually seeps into the soil.

If a home uses a septic system, always have the system inspected by a qualified septic system company who can alert you to any major problems that may be looming. Septic system problems can be expensive, so it is always better to identify them before you close; you may be able to get the seller to make the necessary repairs at their expense.

POOL INSPECTION

If the home has a swimming pool, have a pool professional inspect the pool and pool equipment for major problems. Major pool repairs are expensive, so it is better to know about them before you close.

MORTGAGES

A mortgage is a fancy word for a loan for the purchase of real property. Real property is defined by land and what is under the surface of the earth as well as above the surface. So, permanent structures such as houses are also considered real property. A mortgage is secured by the real property it was used to purchase. If you fail to make the mortgage payments, the mortgagor (the lender) has the legal right to take possession of the property securing the loan.

> **Tip:** While the long-term financial benefits of owning a home are very high, be careful not to rush into buying a home. Timing is everything. Buying when housing prices and/or interest rates are high can yield a very negative effect.

Getting your first home loan (mortgage) can also be a daunting task unless you are familiar with the process. The following items will hopefully help you understand the process a little better:

How much do you qualify for?

Most mortgage lenders use a formula to determine the loan amount they are willing to loan you. This formula will be based primarily on a percentage of your income, but they will also consider your other debts. This is a great reason to stay in control of your credit card debt as discussed above. You may have adequate annual income to qualify for the home of your dreams, but if your other debts such as school loans, car loans, and credit card debt are too high, you may not qualify for the amount you need. This may be true even if your credit score is adequately high (see credit reports and credit scores section). Consult a mortgage loan officer at a bank or mortgage lending company for assistance in determining your qualified loan amount.

In most cases, the loan officer will provide you with a prequalification letter stating in writing their commitment to lend you up to a specified amount. Most selling agents will require this letter with your offer to avoid wasting their client's time with unqualified buyers. Having this letter ahead of time will let you know not only your price range limit, but will also save you time when you find that perfect home and need to move quickly.

How much can you afford?

How much you can afford is similar, but not necessarily the same as, how much you qualify for. It is possible that a loan company will qualify you for an amount, but you may not be comfortable with the size of the mortgage payments. Just because a loan company's formula says you can afford the home, does not mean you can. Only you can decide how much you can afford.

WHAT TO EXPECT DURING THE HOME BUYING PROCESS?

After you've made the offer, put up your earnest money, and signed the contract, now the fun (not really) begins. Once the contract is sent to your lender, you will need to complete several tasks.

Even though your lender has already pre-qualified you for a loan of a certain amount, that was only based on some basic information and formulas. Now they will do their due diligence to be sure everything about you and the property checks out before they close on the property.

This due diligence will include gathering all your financial information including bank balances to verify you have adequate funds to close, sources of income to verify that you are still employed and your salary, assets you own, liabilities (debts) you owe and the monthly payments required on those debts, etc.

The lender will also make sure the property value is adequate to secure the loan amount which includes an appraisal by an appraisal company of their choice. Also, all the legal boxes will be checked such as having a title company perform a title search on the property. A title search is performed to be sure no one has a lien against the property that would place restrictions on the lender's collateral (the property) for the loan. Collateral is a tangible asset used as security for a loan. In other words, the collateral is used by the lender to recoup their money if you default on the loan. They can sell the collateral to recoup their funds. Since the home and land is the collateral securing a mortgage, they want to be certain that they are first in line to claim the collateral in the event of a default.

Understanding interest rates and APR

Every mortgage loan comes with an Annual Percentage Rate (APR) that determines the principal and interest amount of your monthly payment. I will be covering other components of a monthly mortgage payment below, so for now, I will only discuss the APR. Mortgage interest rates fluctuated widely in recent years (this is being written in 2024) so it will depend on where we are in that cycle, based on the health of the U.S. economy. Part of your decision whether to buy a home at a certain time will be based on where interest rates are at that time. Every percentage point in the APR will have a huge effect on your monthly payment, so that will determine affordability. You can use mortgage calculators on the internet to calculate the principal and interest portion of your monthly payment.

There are two major types of mortgage loans that are important to understand:

- Fixed-rate mortgages – the interest rate on the loan remains the same throughout the life of the loan. For example, if you get a 30-year, fixed-rate mortgage with a 6% APR, the principal and interest portion of your monthly payment will remain the same throughout the life of the loan. Most people prefer fixed-rate mortgages because of their predictability.

- Adjustable-Rate Mortgages (ARM) – when mortgage interest rates are high, many potential homebuyers become priced out of the market, i.e., they can't afford the monthly payment because of high interest rates. To accommodate these buyers many mortgage companies offer ARM loans. ARM loans let you start with a much lower interest rate than the prevailing market rate for fixed rate loans, but after the initial rate period, the rate can be adjusted upward to better reflect the rate market at that time. For example, if current fixed-rate mortgages are running around 7%, you might be offered an ARM loan that starts out at 2% APR for 3, 5, 7 or even 10 years. After the initial rate period expires the APR can be adjusted upward at regular intervals such as every 6-months or every year, until the rate is closer to fixed-rates at that time.

WARNING!! ARM loans can be useful in the right situations, but they can also be very dangerous for the wrong buyer. It is beyond the scope of this guide to fully explain the dangers of ARM loans, but be very careful and do your homework before agreeing to an ARM loan.

DOWN PAYMENTS

Every mortgage loan requires a minimum lump sum down payment of some amount based on the size of the loan, the type of the loan, and the lender's own requirements. Without getting into the details of different loan types here, at a high level, required minimum down payments range between 3.5% and 20%, but the typical percentages are between 5% and 10%.

One of the first financial verifications performed by your lender will be ensuring you have adequate funds for the down payment and other closing costs. Check with a loan officer to determine the required down payment amount or percentage. Having this information well ahead of time will help you with your savings goals so you will be ready when the right property comes along.

MONTHLY PAYMENT

Your monthly payment will be a combination of principal, interest, taxes, and insurance. Below I will provide a brief explanation of each of these components.

- Payment components
  - Principal – the portion of the mortgage payment that applies to the loan balance. The early payments in the term of the loan have a small portion applied to principal. Each subsequent payment has a slightly larger principal amount.

  - Interest – the portion of the mortgage payment that applies only to the interest that has accrued on the outstanding balance of the loan since the last payment. Because the loan balance is highest in the earliest years, the portion of each payment at the beginning of the mortgage will be mostly interest. The interest portion of each subsequent payment will be reduced by a small amount as the balance decreases.

- PMI or MIP (FHA) – mortgage insurance which insures the loan amount against default. Depending on the percentage of the down payment you put down, your loan-to-value (LTV) may be too high for the lender's comfort level. LTV is the ratio of the loan amount to the appraised value of the home. For example, if you purchase a home for $200,000, put down 10% or $20,000, and borrow the remaining $180,000, then your LTV will be $180,000/$200,000 or 90%. If you were to default on the loan and the lender is forced to repossess the home, they need to sell the home for at least $180,000 to recoup their total investment. At 90% LTV, the lender's risk level is high, so their ability to recoup 100% of their investment is less likely than a lower LTV. Most lenders prefer the LTV to be below 80%, and some lenders prefer below 75%. When the LTV is above the lender's preferred threshold, most lenders require the buyer to pay for Private Mortgage Insurance (PMI) in addition to the collateral. Mortgage Insurance Premium (MIP) is the same as PMI, except for FHA loans. FHA is a special loan type that requires a smaller down payment (3.5%) than most conventional loans.

- Escrows

  - Homeowner's insurance – All homeowners want to insure their home against loss due to fire, earthquakes, floods, etc., so the home can be repaired or replaced. Many homeowners opt to split their annual premium into smaller parts and add it to their monthly mortgage payment. With this option, the mortgage company places this amount in an escrow account, then pays the premium for you when it becomes due.

- Property Taxes - as with homeowner's insurance, many homeowners opt to split their annual property taxes into small portions to add to their monthly mortgage payment. The mortgage company places the amount into escrow to be paid on the buyer's behalf when property taxes become due.

Tip: Be sure to fully understand all the parts of your mortgage payment. Ask your real estate agent to provide an estimate of total payment including principal, interest, taxes, and insurance before you make an offer.

REFINANCING YOUR MORTGAGE

As mentioned above, mortgage interest rates fluctuate widely over time. If you find yourself in a high interest rate loan and rates drop substantially, you may consider refinancing your mortgage to take advantage of the lower rates. However, be careful to do your research before rushing to refinance. Many refinances result in closing costs that can amount to several thousand dollars.

Some mortgage companies offer refinances with low or no closing costs, so look at the fine print to be sure it makes good financial sense. Some companies may charge closing costs and simply roll these costs into the new loan. While this may help you by not requiring you to pay these costs out of pocket, it is hardly the same as zero closing costs. While your new payment amount may be lower, which is the main reason you want to refinance, the transaction will result in a higher loan balance (how much you need to repay) than before the refinance. This is not always a bad thing, but if you can get a lower rate, a lower payment, and no additional balance, that is much better. Do the math or find someone who can help you decide if the refinance is worth the associated costs. Some questions to ask are:

- Is the difference between the old and new rate enough to justify the refinance, especially if costs are involved?

- If closing costs will be associated with the refinance, how long will it take to recoup those costs with the monthly payment savings?

- If the time required to recoup the costs is multiple years, do you expect to keep the house for at least that long? If not, it makes no sense to refinance.

HOME EQUITY LOAN/LINE OF CREDIT

When your home has accumulated sufficient equity, you may want or need to borrow against that equity for emergencies or any need you deem important. Many loan companies offer Home Equity Lines of Credit or HELOCs that allow you to borrow against this equity.

Different companies have different requirements, but typically, they may be willing to loan you up to 75% of your equity. Once you borrow against this equity, this is treated as a separate loan with its own interest rate, term, and payment amount.

Like other forms of credit and debt, care must be exercised not to get yourself into more debt than you can handle. Not only will your total payments increase with the HELOC, but you will also no longer have the same equity in your home. Equity is one of the ways you build your net worth toward a secure future. When you sell a home in anticipation of buying another home later, the amount of equity you have in the home you are selling becomes a larger amount available to invest in your next home. If your home's value has increased (as homes usually do over time), you will likely be able to put a larger down payment on your next home, allowing you to lower your overall payment, afford a more expensive home, or both. If you erode your equity by borrowing too much against it, you will lose these potential benefits.

HOME MAINTENANCE

Some of the hidden costs of home ownership are the maintenance items that are easy to forget. But to maintain your home's value, you need to keep up with needed maintenance. Here are some of the things you'll need to take care of if you own a home:

- Yard work – if you aren't accustomed to doing your own yardwork, you will need to learn how or hire someone to do it for you. Most neighborhoods will have certain minimum requirements such as mowing, but even if yours has no formal requirements such as from a Homeowner's Association (HOA), you don't want to be the person on the street that is bringing down everyone else's property values, as well as your own.

- Pest control – you will need to treat your home for pests such as insects, rodents, and other pests that can damage your home and jeopardize your health. You can hire a pest control company to treat your home for you, or you can do it yourself. Online companies will provide the chemicals you need to treat your home yourself. Depending on the part of the country you live in, this self-treatment may be adequate.

- Gutter cleaning – depending on the part of the country you live in and the number of leaf-shedding trees near your home, you will need to clean debris out of your gutters at least once a year. Failure to do so can result in gutter damage, damage to the soffits and facia attached to the gutters, as well as foundation damage. This damage will result in costly repairs, or if not repaired, a reduction of your home's value.

- Roofing – depending on how new your roof is, you may not have to worry about this item for a long time. However, your roof may sustain some damage from high winds, hail, falling tree limbs, or other natural causes. Address these repairs in a timely manner to avoid further damage to the roof or leaks inside the home. Roof repairs should be left to a qualified contractor or handyman.

13 TAXES & TAX RETURNS

O ne of the most mysterious aspects of adulting is preparing a tax return. When you first leave home, you may not be experienced in completing your own tax return because either your parent or guardian did it for you, or your annual income up to that point wasn't high enough to require you to file.

For the 2023 tax year, you only need to file a federal tax return if your gross income is at least $13,850, so many young adults starting their first job out of college may not have had to file in the past. Unfortunately, an automatic reminder doesn't pop up on your phone the first time you are required to file, you are just expected to know.

Not only have many never filed in the past, but they have only heard horror stories about filing taxes from their parents or others who also know very little about doing their own taxes. So, along with the mystery, comes the mythology about how difficult it is to do your own tax return. This portion of the guide is not intended to explain every aspect of doing a complicated tax return, which some tax returns are, but rather to demystify the process and direct you to some resources that will simplify the process.

The fact is, a new taxpayer's return can likely be done in a matter of minutes.

13.1 DIY Tax Returns

If you want to try doing your tax return on your own, good for you. Taxpayers whose taxable income is less than $100,000 and filing a single or joint return with no dependents, can use the 1040-EZ tax form. The 1040-EZ is designed to allow qualifying taxpayers to file quickly and easily. Before I show you the form and provide you with some sample numbers, let me define the terms I just used in this paragraph:

- Taxable income – the portion of your income that is eligible to be taxed. This is usually calculated as your gross pay minus any non-taxable deductions such as 401(k) contributions, FSA contributions, standard or itemized deductions, etc.

- Taxpayer – any U.S. worker earning the minimum gross income for their filing status.

- Single filer – if you are single (not married) and only filing a tax return for your own income, your filing status is Single.

Tip: Try one of the online DIY tax programs before you pay someone to do your taxes for you. They are free for most simple tax returns, so you really don't have anything to lose, and everything to gain.

- Joint filer - if you are married and filing a tax return for both you and your spouse on the same return, your filing status is Married Filing Jointly.

- Dependents – while exceptions may apply, dependents are usually children or others for whom you provide more than 50% of their support.

As mentioned earlier, anyone working in the U.S. with a gross income of at least $13,850 for single filers, or $27,700 for filing jointly (with a spouse), is required to file an individual tax return with the Internal Revenue Service (IRS). "Individual" for this purpose is defined as a person, as opposed to an entity such as business.

The tax year for individuals is always a calendar year (January – December). Every employer in the U.S. is required to provide each employee with a W-2 form in January of the year following the previous tax year, e.g., January of 2024 for the 2023 tax year. The W-2 shows how much the employee earned, along with how much federal and state (if applicable) income taxes were withheld from the employee's pay. If you qualify to use form 1040-EZ, the W-2 form is the primary, and in most cases, the only, tax document you will need to file your tax return.

All individual taxpayers must file their tax return by April 15th of the year following the prior tax year. If April 15th falls on a Saturday or Sunday, the tax due date will be the following Monday. Failure to file your tax return by the due date can result in late payment penalties.

Below is a sample W-2 form:

22222	**a** Employee's social security number 123-45-6789		OMB No. 1545-0008		
b Employer identification number (EIN) 99-9283765			**1** Wages, tips, other compensation 47,500.00	**2** Federal income tax withheld 4,321.00	
c Employer's name, address, and ZIP code ABC COMPANY, INC 123 MAIN STREET ANYWHERE, AL 34567			**3** Social security wages 50,000.00	**4** Social security tax withheld 3,100.00	
			5 Medicare wages and tips 50,000.00	**6** Medicare tax withheld 725.00	
			7 Social security tips	**8** Allocated tips	
d Control number 45A-R9854-87			**9**	**10** Dependent care benefits	
e Employee's first name and initial Last name Suff. JOSEPH JONES 345 HOLIDAY LANE MYTOWN, CT 97836			**11** Nonqualified plans	**12a**	
			13 Statutory employee ☐ Retirement plan ☒ Third-party sick pay ☐	**12b**	
			14 Other	**12c**	
				12d	
f Employee's address and ZIP code					

15 State Employer's state ID number	**16** State wages, tips, etc.	**17** State income tax	**18** Local wages, tips, etc.	**19** Local income tax	**20** Locality name
CT 77-9384756	47,500.00	2,850.00			

Form **W-2** Wage and Tax Statement   **2024**   Department of the Treasury—Internal Revenue Service
Copy 1—For State, City, or Local Tax Department

In the sample W-2 above, you will find all the information necessary to file a tax return using the 1040-EZ form.

Nearly every major tax software provider offers a free version for filers who have basic returns and for those who qualify to use the 1040-EZ form. These tax software programs are designed for people who have little or no experience filing taxes, so don't be afraid to give it a try. Here is a list of some of the major tax prep programs available online:

- TurboTax
- TaxAct
- FreeTaxUSA
- H & R Block

- Liberty Tax
- TaxSlayer

With any of these programs, you can select the interview method of answering the software's questions to determine how to prepare your tax return. They make it so simple anyone can do it.

13.2 Using a Tax Service

If you still don't want to do your own tax return using one of the free software programs above, you can use a popular tax preparation service. Many of these companies have offices where they can prepare your return while you wait. Many of these are in larger retail stores like Walmart. Below is a list of just a few of the tax preparation companies:

- H & R Block
- Jackson Hewitt
- Liberty Tax

Many of these popular tax preparation companies offer tax refund advances, so you can get your tax refund when you get your return prepared. Of course, this feature will come with a fee or a percentage of your refund, but you can decide if it is worth it to you or not.

By using either an online software solution or an in-person tax preparation service, you can file your return electronically so it gets to the IRS and/or your state revenue office immediately. If you are getting a tax refund, filing electronically will speed up the process.

I've mentioned tax refunds a couple of times already, but I need to make sure you know that getting a refund is not guaranteed. Let me explain how taxes, tax withholding, and tax refunds work. For this illustration, I will only discuss federal taxes.

- When you start a new job, you are required to fill out a W-4 form. The W-4 tells your employer how to withhold federal taxes from your paycheck.

- The U.S. tax system is a pay-as-you-go system which means your employer holds back some of your pay each pay period and sends it to the IRS on your behalf. Your employer knows how much to withhold based on the information you provide on your W-4 form.

- The W-4 form is a simple form if you understand how it works. For most young adults starting their first job, the form only needs to know your filing status. Filing status is one of the following:

  - Single
  - Married Filing Jointly
  - Head of Household

By selecting which of these filing statuses you plan to use when you file your taxes, your employer will know how to estimate your tax withholdings. However, this is not the same as the actual amount of tax you will pay; this is only an estimate for withholding purposes.

Your actual taxes will be calculated when you prepare your tax return, and the total tax liability may be more or less than the estimated tax withheld from your pay. Many taxpayers receive a tax refund instead of owing more taxes because the calculations overestimated their withholdings. So, as much as politicians would like you to think they are giving you a tax refund out of the goodness of their heart, you are just getting refunded the amount you overpaid. It is your money, not a gift from the government.

While most people like the idea of receiving this bonus each year, you are just giving the government an interest-free loan. In a perfect world, your tax withholdings would match your tax return so you owe nothing and receive nothing when you file your taxes.

Please note that in most states, you will also need to file a state income tax return. Only Alaska, Florida, Nevada, South Dakota, Tennessee, Texas, and Wyoming do not currently have state income tax. All the tax prep software programs and services listed above can take care of your state return when you prepare your federal return.

14 GLOSSARY OF TERMS

1-2-3

1040-EZ Form	An IRS tax form designed for simple tax returns.
401(k)	A tax-advantage retirement account sponsored by employers for employees.

A

Accrue (Student Loans)	Accumulate or receive.
Annual Fee (Credit Cards)	An amount charged each year for the use of a credit card.
Annual Percentage Rate (APR)	The amount of interest charged per year for the use of loaned funds.

B

Bank Fees	A charge for the use and maintenance of a bank account.
Beneficiary	A person who benefits from something, especially a trust, will, or life insurance policy.
Benefits (Employee)	Any kind of tangible or intangible compensation given to employees apart from base wages or base salaries. Examples are job benefits such as insurance (including medical, dental, and life), stock options, and cell phone plans.
Bills	Charges for services rendered (usually monthly) such as utilities, and insurance premiums.
Bi-Weekly	Every two weeks.

Brake Fluid	A type hydraulic fluid used in a braking system on an automobile.
Budget	A financial plan that compares income to expenses.

C

Check Engine Codes	An alpha-numeric diagnostic code generated from an automobile when the check engine light appears.
Check Engine Light	A dashboard icon shaped like a car engine that indicates a problem with the engine.
Checking Accounts	A bank account meant to have high-volume transactions such as payments by check.
Clear Title	A car title that has no lienholder; a fully paid vehicle title.
Closing Costs	All the costs associated with closing a home loan including down payment, loan points, attorney fees, survey fees, title search, and title insurance.
Collateral	A tangible asset used to back a loan, i.e., the asset will be taken by the creditor if the person receiving the loan defaults on the loan payments.
Collision (Insurance)	Auto insurance that covers damage resulting from moving accidents.
Comprehensive (Insurance)	Auto insurance that covers damage resulting from non-moving accidents, e.g., tree limbs, hail, and other natural causes.
Consumer Loans	A loan other than home loans for things like home improvements, cars, and personal expenditures.
Conventional Banks	A bank with physical branches.
Conventional Oil (Auto)	Motor oil made from real petroleum products.
Co-sign	Having another person sign a loan contract with you for added security to the creditor.

Credit History	The accumulation of a person's credit transactions over time.
Credit Protection	A service that helps you repair your credit and recover losses.
Credit Report	A report of your credit history.
Credit Report Monitoring	A service that keeps an eye on your credit report for potential unauthorized transactions.
Credit Reporting Companies	The three bureaus where credit transactions are reported, and credit scores are calculated.
Credit Score	A calculated three-digit number based on multiple credit factors. The score attempts to provide potential creditors with a single score that represents your credit worthiness.

D

Damage Deposit	An amount paid at the start of a rental agreement to cover any damages to the rental space. Depending on how much damage is found when you leave, part or all the deposit may be returned.
Death Benefit	When you have life insurance, the death benefit is the amount paid out to your beneficiaries when you die.
Debit Card	Like a credit card except the funds come directly from your checking account balance.
Deductible (Insurance)	In the insurance world, a deductible is the amount you pay before the insurance company pays. In auto insurance, this is paid for each event (accident). For health insurance this is usually on an annual basis, i.e., once you reach your total deductible for the year, you don't pay any more for that year.

Deductions (Paycheck)	Any amount subtracted from your gross pay such as federal and state income taxes, social security taxes, insurance premiums, 401(k) contributions, etc.
Default	When a person stops making the required payments on a loan for an extended time, they have defaulted.
Deferment (Student Loans)	When a student loan servicing company allows you to stop making payments for a period of time.
Dependents	For tax purposes, a dependent is any qualifying child or relative of the taxpayer. Some examples of dependents include a child, stepchild, brother, sister, or parent.
Deposit (Utilities)	An amount paid to a utility provider such as electric, gas, or water.
Direct Deposit	The term used when an employer has your paycheck deposited into your checking account instead of giving you a physical check.
Down Payment	A lump sum amount paid toward the purchase of something before a loan is received. Down payments are most often used for automobile and home loans.
Due Diligence	Reasonable steps taken by a person to satisfy a legal requirement, especially in buying or selling something.
Due Diligence Period	In some states, when purchasing real estate, a stated number of days is allowed for the buyer to perform due diligence. This time is called the "due diligence period." See Due Diligence.

E

Earnest Money	A payment of funds when an offer to purchase real estate is made.

Electronic Filing	The process of sending your tax return directly to the IRS over the internet.
Emissions Inspection	In some states, an annual inspection to determine if your vehicle is producing too many pollutants from the exhaust system (emissions system).
Engine Coolant (Antifreeze)	A fluid put into your car's cooling system to help regulate the temperature of the engine. While often referred to as coolant, this fluid also serves to prevent the engine from freezing.
Equity	Your ownership portion of an asset calculated as (Fair Market Value - Amount you owe = Equity).
Escrow	Amounts paid by you but held by a third party until needed. In this guide, escrow is referring to amounts you pay as part of your mortgage payment for property taxes and homeowner's insurance that are held by the mortgage company until those amounts become due.
Expense	Amounts you pay out for goods or services rendered. This term is used in this guide in the context of making a budget. You subtract expenses from your income to see if anything is left.

F

FAFSA (Student Loans)	An acronym for Free Application for Federal Student Aid. The FAFSA application is required each year if you wish to receive federal student aid.
Fair Market Value	The amount most people would be willing to pay for an asset such as a house or condominium.

Federal Housing Administration (FHA)	The Federal Housing Administration (FHA) is part of the U.S. Department of Housing and Urban Development. The FHA provides home loans called FHA loans that have a lower down payment requirement and require MIP insurance as part of your payment.
Filing Status	For federal and state tax purposes, you must choose whether to file as a single individual, jointly with a spouse, married filing separately, or as head of household. These designations are called "filing status" and determine both your tax withholdings and tax payments.
Flexible Spending Account (FSA)	An employee benefit offered by most employers that allows an employee to set aside tax-free funds in an account to be used for medical and medical related expenses.
Fluids	The various liquids in your automobile that allow it to perform properly. Examples are motor oil, and transmission, brake, and windshield washer fluids.
Forbearance (Student Loans)	When a student loan servicing company allows you to stop making payments for up to 12 months.

G

Good Faith	A phrase that means "to act honestly, and with sincerity of intent." In this guide, I used this term when explaining earnest money as a show of good faith.

Grace Period	For many loan contracts, rental agreements, and other similar agreements, while the stated monthly due date may be the first day of the month, typically, a few days are specified beyond that date during which you are allowed to make a payment without being charged with a late payment fee. This is referred to as the grace period. For example, if your rent is due on the 1st, but has a 10-day grace period, you can pay by the 10th without a late fee.
Gross Amount	Used in this guide to refer to paychecks, it is the amount you earned during the pay period before any deductions are subtracted. For example, if you make $15/hour and you worked 40 hours during the pay period, your gross pay amount is $600, before taxes, insurance, and other amounts are deducted.

H

Health Insurance Premiums	The term "premium" is the insurance industry's word for the cost of an insurance policy. For health insurance, it is usually the amount deducted from each paycheck to pay for your health insurance coverage.
Home Equity Line of Credit (HELOC)	When you have equity (see "equity" in this glossary) in your home, you may be able to borrow against it. This loan is often referred to as a Home Equity Line of Credit or HELOC.
Home Loan (Mortgage)	A type of loan used to purchase real estate (land, houses) where the property serves as collateral for the loan (see collateral).
Homeowner's Insurance	A type of insurance that protects a homeowner against losses due to fire, natural disasters (earthquakes, hail, tornadoes, floods) and other causes.

I

Identity Theft	When someone illegally pretends to be you for the purpose of stealing from you, usually in the form of taking out credit cards or loans in your name.
Income	The amounts you receive from working or investments. For employed people, usually your paycheck.
Income Taxes	Amounts paid to federal, state, and local governments based on the amount of income you earn.
Income-Driven Repayment Plan (Student Loans)	A payment plan based on your level of income. If your earnings are too low to make standard payment amounts, you may qualify for a reduced payment amount based on your income level.
Individual Retirement Account (IRA)	An investment account that allows you to save for your retirement using pre-tax dollars. The taxes are deferred until you withdraw the funds for retirement.
Inspection (Auto)	Some states require automobiles to undergo an inspection each year to ensure it is safe to drive.
Installment Loan	In the context of loan payments, "installment" simply means to pay in equal monthly payments (installments). An "installment loan" is a loan where you are allowed to make monthly payments to pay off the balance.
Insurance, Auto	A type of insurance for the use of an automobile. All states have legal minimum requirements called liability insurance, but many owners also carry both collision and comprehensive (see definitions) coverage.
Insurance Agent	A person authorized and licensed to acquire insurance policies on your behalf.

Insurance, Health	A type of insurance meant to protect you when you have medical expenses.
Insurance, Life	A type of insurance meant to protect your family against the loss of your income when you die. Life insurance pays your beneficiaries an amount (death benefit) upon your death.
Interest	An amount paid for the use of someone else's money in the form of a loan. Usually represented by a percentage paid on the outstanding balance each year, i.e. 6% per year.
Internal Revenue Service (IRS)	The part of the U.S. Treasury Department that handles income tax collection.
Itemized Deductions	When preparing an individual tax return using form 1040, some taxpayers can list (itemize) all their qualifying expenses that can be deducted from their gross earnings when calculating their taxable Income. Examples of qualifying expenses include some medical expenses, interest, and points to purchase a first or second home, charitable contributions, etc.

J

Joint Filer	When a taxpayer combines his/her income with that of a spouse or domestic partner for tax purposes. This is one of the filing statuses (see definition).
Jumper Cables	A pair of wire cables designed to connect the batteries of two vehicles together for the purpose of jump-starting (see jump start) a vehicle with a dead battery.
Jump Start	When your automobile won't start because the battery is dead, you may be able use the battery of another vehicle to start yours. This is called "jump-starting." To jump start

a vehicle, you must have a set of jumper cables.

L

Landlord	The person or company who owns and/or manages a rental property. You pay your monthly rent to your landlord.
Late Fees	A penalty amount assessed for making any scheduled payment later than the contractual payment date. Late fees can apply to rent payments, credit card and other loan payments, utilities, etc.
Lease Agreement	A type of rental contract that specifies the term of the agreement. The term "lease" usually refers to a longer time frame than a simple rental agreement, e.g., a one-year lease.
Liability (Insurance)	The term "liability" in the context of auto insurance is a legal action against you for some action deemed to be your fault. For example, if you have an auto accident deemed to be your fault, you could be sued by the injured party for damages. That would be a liability to you, so liability insurance protects you against this.
Lien (Auto)	The term "lien" means a right to keep possession of property belonging to another person until a debt owed by that person is discharged. When a creditor loans you money to buy a car, that car becomes the collateral (see definition) for that loan. To make that claim against the car legal and binding, the loan company places a lien against the vehicle's title to show that they have a claim on the property.

Lienholder (Auto)	The party who places a lien (see definition) on an asset.
Loan Forgiveness (Student Loans)	In the context of student loans, loan forgiveness is when your student loan debt is removed so you no longer must pay it.
Loan Officer	A person at a bank or other financial institution trained and authorized to make loans to the public.
Loan to Value (LTV)	A ratio of (Amount of Loan to Fair Market Value). This ratio measures the lienholder's relative amount of risk in the event the person receiving the loan defaults on the loan payments.
Lockout Service	A service offered by many roadside assistance plans where a locksmith will be sent to help you get into your vehicle if you accidentally lock yourself out.
Locksmith	A person trained to pick locks, make keys, and open locked spaces.

M

Minimum Payment (Credit Cards)	The least (minimum) amount acceptable by a creditor to satisfy your monthly credit card payment. This amount is always printed on your monthly statement/bill.
Monthly	Any payment made one time per month. This can refer to payments you make to others, as well as the frequency in which you get paid.
Mortgage Insurance Payment (MIP)	A type of insurance that protects the creditor on an FHA home loan against potential default.
Mortgage Loan	A type of loan used to purchase real estate (land, houses) where the property serves as collateral for the loan (see collateral).
Motor Oil	The lubricant used in car engines to prevent wear of metal parts as well as overheating.

N

Net Amount	An amount after all required or optional deductions are subtracted.
Notarize	To have a physical signature witnessed by a notary public.
Notary Public	A person trained, licensed, and bonded who can be an official witness on official documents.

O

Offer	A legal term for a proposed amount and terms to purchase some asset. In the context of this guide, "offer" refers to the official offer to purchase a home.
Oil Pressure	Every automobile must have an adequate amount of motor oil. When oil in an engine either leaks out or is burned up (both resulting from malfunctions), the engine does not have enough pressure to keep engine parts adequately lubricated. This term was used in this guide in the discussion of fluid checks and dashboard problem indicators.
Oil Type (Auto)	Motor oil types are indicated by numbers and letters such as 10W-30 that indicate the temperatures they are rated for in summer and winter. These numbers indicate the viscosity (fluidness) of the oil. "Oil type" can also refer to what the lubricant is made from, e.g., conventional (made of natural petroleum products) and synthetic (artificially manufactured lubricants).
Online Banking	A bank that only has an online presence, i.e., they do not have physical branches you can walk into.

Overdraft Fees	When you try to spend more than you have in your checking account, most banks will cover the payment for you but may charge you a penalty (fee). Spending more than you have is called an overdraft.

P

Pads (Brakes)	In an automobile's braking system, most modern vehicles use pads and rotors. The rotor is a disk that turns with the wheel and tire. The pads press against the rotor to stop the vehicle.
Pay slip, Paystub	The details attached (associated) with your check. With a physical paycheck, it is a stub or slip attached to the check that provides the details of how the net pay was derived from Gross Pay to Net Pay.
Pet Deposit	Many rental agreements require an additional deposit if you have a pet due to the high potential for pet related damages.
Policy	A term used for an insurance contract.
Power Steering Fluid	A type of hydraulic fluid that allows your power steering to work properly.
Premium (Insurance)	The term used by insurance companies for the cost of an insurance policy.
Pre-tax	When dollars are allowed to be used "pre-tax", it means before the money is taxed. What this means for you is those dollars are not reported on your W-2 form as income, so it is not taxed when you file your tax return. See the examples under 401(k) and FSA in this guide.
Principal and Interest	Each payment against an installment loan of any kind is made up of two parts: a part that goes toward principal which is the loan balance, and a part that goes toward paying the interest for using that money.

Private Mortgage Insurance (PMI)	A type of insurance that protects the creditor on a conventional home loan against potential default.
Probationary Period	A time at the beginning of a new job when you are not eligible for some benefits. The two most common examples are 401(k) and health insurance benefits.
Proof of Insurance (Auto)	A physical or digital card showing that you have insurance on your vehicle.
Property Tax	All real estate is taxed by the state and local governments where the property is located. Property taxes are assessed based on the value of the land and improvements (buildings) on that land.

R

Real Estate	Land and everything that exists above and below the surface of the land. This usually includes buildings such as houses, barns, etc., but also includes water and mineral rights.
Refinancing	The process of having a loan restructured usually to lower the interest but can also include changing other terms. Most often used in reference to home loans.
Registration (Auto)	The document accompanying your physical license plate (tag) that shows that your vehicle is properly recorded with the state in which you live and that registration is current. When a police officer asks for your registration, he wants to see the paper registration that came with your tag.
Rental Agreement	A type of contract that specifies the terms of the agreement to rent something, usually a house or apartment. The term "rental" can be the same as "lease" but sometimes refers to a shorter time frame than a lease

	agreement. Rental agreements can sometimes be month-to-month, where leases are more often for a long-term agreement.
Renter's Insurance	When you are living in a rented space like an apartment or rental house, you can insure your personal property like furniture, jewelry, musical instruments, etc., against theft, or damage and loss due to fire, flood, and other natural events. This is called renter's insurance.
Return on Investment (ROI)	The incremental increase in an asset's value over time. If you invest $1,000, and after one year the value of that investment is $1,100, your return amount is $100, and your return percentage is 10%. ROI is most often expressed as a percentage of the original investment.
Rewards Credit Cards	A credit card that pays you cashback rewards or miles that can be used for travel.
Risk (Insurance)	The relative probability of losing an asset. In insurance of any type, the insurance company weighs its relative risk of losing money if they must pay claims, and charges premiums based on that level of risk.
Roadside Assistance	A prepaid plan with a company who will handle roadside emergencies for you. These plans always include towing services, and often also cover locksmith services, out-of-gas situations, flat tire service, and jump-starting.
Roth IRA	Like the standard IRA except you contribute after-tax (already taxed) dollars into a Roth. So, while you do not reap the benefit of tax-deferral in the current tax year as you do with a standard IRA, all investment growth

	on your contributions is tax-free even when you withdraw them at retirement.
Rotors	In an automobile's braking system, most modern vehicles use pads and rotors. The rotor is a disk that turns with the wheel and tire. The pads press against the rotor to stop the vehicle.

S

Savings Accounts	A bank account intended for low-volume transactions such as a few deposits and withdrawals each month. Designed primarily as a savings instrument.
Semi-Monthly	When something occurs two times per month such as a payday. Semi-monthly paydays are often on the 15th and the last day of each month.
Septic System	A septic system is used with homes that are too far removed from a city or town to be connected to a municipal sewer system. A septic system is made up of a large underground holding tank connected to field lines which are a series of underground pipes running through the yard of the home. When sinks are drained, toilets are flushed, showers are drained, etc., the water travels into the holding tank first. Then, that water drains into the field lines and eventually seeps into the soil.
Short-term Disability	A type of insurance that protects you from loss of income for a short period of time, usually between 3 - 6 months. This insurance is usually paid out when an employee has a health issue that keeps them from working temporarily.

Simplified Employee Plan (SEP)	A type of IRA designed for self-employed individuals.
Single Filer	When a taxpayer files an income tax return for his/her own income only. This is one of the filing statuses (see definition).
Social Security Taxes	A mandatory tax paid by all U.S. employees and matched by employers to fund the U.S. Social Security System paid to U.S. citizens after the minimum age of 62.
Standard Deduction	When you file your taxes, you are allowed a stated amount of deductions from your gross income to arrive at your taxable income. For each filing status (single, joint, head of household) there is a set amount that a taxpayer can deduct without itemizing their deductions. This amount is called the standard deduction.
Student Loans	Loans funded and managed by the federal government to assist U.S. citizens in getting a college education.
Survey	During the home purchasing process, a survey is when the physical boundaries (property lines) are checked for accuracy with the records for that property.
Synthetic Oil (Auto)	A motor oil made from chemically produced components rather than natural petroleum products.
T	
Tag (Auto)	The physical license plate (tag) that every automobile is required to have on the rear of the vehicle (some states require a tag on the back and front).
Tax Advantaged	A term that refers to any savings or investment vehicle that provides some tax benefit to the taxpayer, either currently

and/or in the future. Examples in this guide are 401(k)s, IRAs, and Roth IRAs.

Tax Credit — A tax credit is an amount that you are allowed to subtract dollar-for-dollar from your tax liability. For example, after doing your tax return your calculated tax amount is $3,000. You have a tax credit for installing high efficiency windows during the tax year in the amount of $1,000. You can reduce your tax amount by the full tax credit amount.

Tax Refunds — A repayment of taxes withheld from your pay that exceeds the calculated total tax due on your tax return. For example, you calculate your taxes for the year and your tax amount is $3,000. Your employer withheld $3,500 from your pay for the year, so you will receive a refund of $500.

Tax Withholding — Amounts subtracted from your gross pay each pay period and paid on your behalf to the federal and state tax authorities.

Taxable Income — The amount of your income subject to taxation. This amount is derived from your gross reported income, less qualifying deductions.

Tax-deferred — When the taxation of a portion of your income is delayed (deferred) until a later time, usually at retirement.

Taxes and Fees (Auto) — These terms were used in this guide in the context of automobile tags and titles. When you renew your tags each year and when you get your tag and title for the first time for a new car, you will be charged taxes on the value of the vehicle, and fees to cover the processing of these documents.

Taxpayer	An individual who is subject to taxes on his/her earned and unearned income. On a tax return, it is the individual(s) named on the tax form.
Term Life (Insurance)	A type of life insurance that is for a limited time (term) such as ten years. This is in contrast with whole life insurance which can be in force for the entire (whole) life of the insured.
Tire Pressure	Tires on vehicles have a recommended air pressure printed on the tire. For optimal performance and tire life, you should keep your tire pressure at or near the suggested pressure for that tire. Tire pressure is measured in PSI (pounds per square inch) so a typical PSI on a standard passenger vehicle may be 32 PSI.
Tire Pressure Gauge	A small and inexpensive tool for checking tire pressure on vehicles.
Tire Pressure Monitoring System (TPMS)	Most modern vehicles have a system that monitors tire pressure for you called a Tire Pressure Monitoring System (TPMS). In most passenger vehicles, the only feedback you will receive from the TPMS is a dashboard icon that looks like the profile of a tire (see guide under Tires).
Title (Auto)	Every automotive vehicle must have a document that proves who owns it. That document is called a "Title" and is issued by the state in which the vehicle is tagged and registered.
Towing Service	The primary service provided with a Roadside Assistance plan. A towing service is when a tow truck is sent to your location in the event of a roadside breakdown.

Transmission Fluid	A type of lubricating fluid required in a vehicle's transmission to allow it to work properly.

U

Utilities	A blanket term for all the services you need for a home such as electricity, natural gas or propane, internet service, garbage pickup, and water.

V

Vehicle Identification Number (VIN)	A unique 17-digit alpha-numeric identifier on every vehicle manufactured after 1981.
VIN Decoder	A program that can decipher (decode) information built into a vehicle's VIN. Far more than simply a unique number to identify a vehicle, the VIN can be decoded to indicate country of manufacture, year of manufacture, make, model, and even many of the standard features.
Viscosity	A measure of the thickness or fluidity of a non-solid (liquid) substance. In motor oil, the two numbers such as 10W-30, are indicators of the relative thickness of an oil under certain conditions such as summer and winter temperatures.

W

W-2	A tax form provided by an employer to every employee that reports the employee's income as well as certain tax related deductions like taxes withheld.
W-4	A tax form that every employee is required to complete when first hired to designate how they wish to withhold taxes, i.e., filing status, number of dependents, and additional withholding amount (if needed).

Warranty (Auto)	A type of insurance that covers certain repairs on automobiles. Many new vehicles come with a warranty at no additional cost. Extended warranties can be purchased for vehicles after the original warranty expires.
Weekly	When something occurs every week such as a pay day. Weekly pay days are usually on the same day of the calendar week.
Whole life (Insurance)	A type of life insurance that will remain in force for the insured person's entire (whole) life. This is in contrast with term life insurance which is only for a limited time frame such as ten years.
Windshield Washer Fluid	A window cleaning fluid held in a reservoir that can be sprayed onto the windshield by the driver to clean the windshield.

Y

Year, Make, and Model	Three designations to identify the type of a vehicle. "Year" is the year it was manufactured, "Make" is the brand or company of the vehicle such as Ford, Chevrolet, Mercedes, and "Model" is the type of vehicle manufactured such as Impala, Tahoe, Corvette, etc.

www.ingramcontent.com/pod-product-compliance
Lightning Source LLC
LaVergne TN
LVHW022341080426
835508LV00012BA/1302